Rush-Hour Recipes

Gooseberry Patch
2500 Farmers Dr., #110
Columbus, OH 43235

www.gooseberrypatch.com

1·800·854·6673

Copyright 2011, Gooseberry Patch 978-1-61281-030-0
First Printing, September, 2011

Do you have a tried & true recipe...

tip, craft or memory that you'd like to see featured in a **Gooseberry
Patch** cookbook? Visit our website at **www.gooseberrypatch.com**
to share them with us instantly. If you'd rather jot them down by hand,
use the handy form in the front of this book and send them to...

Gooseberry Patch
Attn: Cookbook Dept.
2500 Farmers Dr., #110
Columbus, OH 43235

Don't forget to include the number of servings your recipe makes,
plus your name, address, phone number and email address.
If we select your recipe, your name will appear right along
with it...and you'll receive a **FREE** copy of the cookbook!

Contents

Dedication

To all of our friends who cherish
sitting down to a home-cooked family
meal...no matter how busy they are!

Appreciation

For taking the time to share your
most delicious homestyle recipes
with us...thanks so much!

5-Ingredient Favorites

Bacon & Cheddar Chicken

Kathy Grashoff
Fort Wayne, IN

Juicy chicken in a savory cheese sauce...yum!

1 T. oil
4 boneless, skinless chicken
   breasts
1/3 c. bacon, chopped

1/2 c. onion, chopped
1/2 c. milk
6 slices American cheese,
   chopped

Heat oil in a large skillet over medium-high heat; add chicken. Cook, turning once, for about 7 to 8 minutes, until golden on both sides and chicken juices run clear when pierced. Transfer chicken to a plate; cover to keep warm. Add bacon to drippings in skillet. Cook and stir over medium heat until crisp, about 2 minutes. Add onion; cook and stir until tender, about 3 minutes. Add milk and cheese; cook and stir until smooth. Return chicken to the skillet along with any juices that have collected on the plate. Turn chicken in sauce to coat. Serve chicken with cheese sauce spooned over it. Makes 4 servings.

Boneless chicken breasts are a terrific choice for speedy meals. They'll cook up even quicker if placed in a large plastic zipping bag and flattened with a meat mallet.

5-Ingredient *Favorites*

Creamed Chicken Over Cornbread

Bobbi Greene
Mount Juliet, TN

This delicious, quick recipe helped stretch the family food budget when our daughter was young and I was a stay-at-home mom. For a change, serve over warm, split biscuits.

8-1/2 oz. pkg. cornbread mix
2 boneless, skinless chicken
   breasts, cut into bite-size
   pieces
2/3 c. water

10-3/4 oz. can cream of chicken
   soup
1 c. milk
1/2 t. pepper

Prepare and bake cornbread mix according to package directions. While cornbread is baking, combine chicken and water in a saucepan. Cook over medium-low heat until chicken is very tender, about 15 minutes; drain. In a separate saucepan, mix soup, milk and pepper; cook over medium heat until hot and creamy. Add chicken to soup mixture and stir to coat; heat through. Cut baked cornbread into squares. Split cornbread squares and top with chicken mixture. Serves 2 to 4.

Keep a notepad on the fridge
to make a note whenever
a pantry staple is used
up...you'll never run out of that
one item you need for dinner.

Preston's Zucchini Stir-Fry

Lisa Ellsworth
Sparta, MO

My husband Preston came up with this delicious dish one day while trying to figure out new ways of dealing with an abundance of zucchini. It's fast, inexpensive and very tasty...even the kids love it!

1 lb. ground beef
1 to 2 zucchini, cut into
  bite-size pieces
1 onion, chopped

1-1/2 c. water
1-1/2 c. instant rice, uncooked
soy sauce or Worcestershire
  sauce to taste

Add beef, zucchini and onion to a skillet. Cook over medium-high heat until beef is browned and vegetables are tender; drain. Add water and rice; bring to a boil. Remove from heat. Cover and let stand until water is absorbed and rice is tender, about 5 minutes. Add desired sauce to taste. Serves 4.

Sausage Orzo Skillet

Julie Lundblad
Chardon, OH

This skillet meal is quick, easy and my whole family likes it! I've tried several flavors of sausage and they're all delicious.

1 lb. ground pork sausage
14-1/2 oz. can beef broth
14-1/2 oz. can stewed tomatoes

1-1/4 c. orzo pasta, uncooked
Optional: Italian seasoning
  to taste

In a skillet over medium heat, brown sausage; drain. Add broth and tomatoes with their juice; bring to a boil. Stir in orzo; sprinkle with Italian seasoning, if using. Cover and simmer for 15 minutes, until orzo is tender. Makes 4 servings.

Save time on kitchen clean-up...always use a spatter screen when frying in a skillet or Dutch oven.

Zucchini Rodeo Casserole

Cindy Brewer
Seguin, TX

We rodeo a lot, so I need a filling meal...and I prefer to fix it in one skillet. Yeehaw, everyone loves this! If your family likes a milder taste, use just half of the enchilada sauce.

2 lbs. ground beef
1 zucchini, shredded or chopped
15-oz. can green enchilada
  sauce
15-oz. can ranch-style beans

cooked rice or taco shells
Garnish: sour cream, shredded
  cheese, diced tomatoes and
  avocado

Brown beef in a skillet over medium heat; drain. Add zucchini, enchilada sauce and beans. Stir well and heat through, about 12 minutes. Serve over cooked rice or in taco shells, with desired toppings. Serves 4 to 6.

Declare a picnic night at home! Just toss a checkered tablecloth on the dinner table and set out paper plates and disposable plastic utensils. Relax and enjoy dinner...no dishes to wash!

Grilled Western Chicken Sandwich

Thomas Campbell
Hopkins, MN

The flavor of this simple sandwich is wonderful. Family & friends will think that there are tons of ingredients in it...only you know there aren't! For a smoky taste, sometimes I use western salad dressing with bacon.

4 boneless, skinless chicken
  breasts
12-oz. bottle western salad
  dressing
1 T. pepper

4 kaiser onion rolls, split and
  toasted
Garnish: 4 lettuce leaves,
  4 thick slices tomato

Place chicken breasts, salad dressing and pepper in a gallon-size plastic zipping bag. Seal bag; shake gently to coat chicken. Refrigerate for 3 hours to overnight. Heat a grill to medium-high, about 350 degrees. Remove chicken from bag; discard marinade. Grill chicken until cooked through and chicken juices run clear when pierced. Place each piece of chicken on a toasted bun bottom; top with lettuce, tomato and top of bun. Makes 4 servings.

A ridged cast-iron grill skillet is handy for grilling on your stovetop whenever it's too cold or rainy to use the grill outdoors.

Chicken Caesar Pita Wraps

Laura Witham
Anchorage, AK

My friends and I used to meet for lunch at a favorite restaurant. I always ordered the chicken Caesar pita sandwich...I really looked forward to it! Over the years, our lunch bunch broke up, so I decided to try making it myself. Now I can enjoy this wrap often. It's quickly becoming my husband's favorite, too.

4 boneless, skinless chicken
    breasts
Montreal steak seasoning
    to taste
3 T. olive oil

1/2 c. Caesar salad dressing
4 pita rounds
Optional: shredded Parmesan
    cheese

With a sharp knife, carefully slice horizontally most of the way through each chicken breast; open up and flatten. Sprinkle one side of chicken with seasoning. Heat oil in a large skillet over medium-high heat. Add chicken to skillet; sprinkle other side with seasoning. Cook until golden on both sides and chicken juices run clear when pierced. Remove chicken from skillet to a cutting board. Let cool briefly; slice into strips and transfer to a bowl. Drizzle salad dressing over chicken; stir to coat well. Microwave pita rounds for 20 to 30 seconds, until warmed. Divide chicken mixture evenly among rounds. Sprinkle with Parmesan cheese, if desired. Serves 4.

When you bring home groceries, label any recipe ingredients before refrigerating so they won't become snacks instead. Label any packages or containers of cheese, veggies and fruit that are intended for between-meal snacking.

Braised Pork Chops

Debora de Faria
The Woodlands, TX

The aroma of these pork chops on the stove brings back memories of my grandmother and mother's kitchens. Both were wonderful cooks! The longer you cook the pork chops, the more tender they become. Serve with mashed potatoes to enjoy the flavorful gravy.

1 c. all-purpose flour
salt and pepper to taste
6 pork chops

3 T. oil
1 c. catsup
2 c. water

In a shallow bowl, mix flour with salt and pepper; dust pork chops completely. Heat oil in a large skillet over medium-high heat. Add pork chops; cook until golden on both sides. Pour catsup over pork chops. Add water to skillet to cover pork chops completely. Cover and cook over low heat for 25 to 30 minutes, turning once or twice, to desired tenderness. Makes 6 servings.

Mashed potatoes are the perfect partner for creamy comfort foods. Make 'em in a jiffy! Quarter potatoes (no peeling required!) and cook in boiling water until tender, 10 to 20 minutes. Drain, mash right in the pot and stir in butter, salt and a little milk to desired consistency.

Stuffed Cube Steaks

Judith Long
Harriman, TN

This is a recipe that I have made for years... my family loves it!
Just add a veggie and voilà, a quick & easy meal.

6-oz. pkg. stuffing mix
.87-oz. pkg. brown gravy mix

4 beef cube steaks
2 to 3 t. oil

Prepare stuffing mix according to package directions, adding a little extra liquid to make it extra moist. Place a heaping spoonful of stuffing on each steak; roll up and secure with wooden toothpicks. Place oil in a large cast-iron skillet over medium-high heat; add stuffed steaks and brown on all sides. Meanwhile, prepare gravy mix according to package directions. When steaks are browned on all sides, add gravy to skillet. Reduce heat; cover and simmer for about 10 minutes, until steaks are tender. Serves 4.

Create a meal plan for one or even two weeks, including all of your favorite quick & easy meals...spaghetti on Monday, chicken pot pie on Tuesday and so forth. It can be very specific or more general. Post it on the fridge along with a shopping list...making dinner will be a snap!

Sausage & Spanish Rice Skillet

Kathy Smith
Cincinnati, OH

My husband and I came up with this tasty recipe. My daughters and grandchildren really enjoy it!

1 lb. smoked pork sausage links, cut into one-inch pieces
2 to 3 t. oil
1-1/2 c. instant rice, uncooked
1-1/2 c. chicken broth
8-oz. jar mild or hot salsa
2 c. shredded Cheddar cheese

In a large skillet over medium-high heat, brown sausage in oil; drain. Meanwhile, prepare rice according to package directions, using broth instead of water. Add rice and salsa to sausage in skillet; sprinkle with cheese. Cover and cook over low heat for a few minutes, until cheese melts. Makes 4 servings.

Curly Noodle Surprise

April Burdette
Parkersburg, WV

This recipe is fast and easy to make. My husband and kids love it.

1 lb. ground beef
1 onion, chopped
1 c. water
2 3-oz. pkgs. beef-flavored ramen noodles, crushed
2 14-1/2 oz. cans diced tomatoes
2 15-1/2 oz. cans kidney or chili beans, drained

In a large skillet over medium heat, brown beef and onion; drain. Stir in water, crushed noodles with seasoning packets, tomatoes with juice and beans. Bring to a boil. Simmer for about 5 minutes, until heated through and noodles are soft. Serves 4.

Laughter is brightest where food is best.

– Irish Proverb

5-Ingredient *Favorites*

Irish Supper

Erin Stamile
Waco, TX

This super-easy recipe was given to me by a friend as a go-to meal.
It's delicious...a household favorite! Serve with some
warm Irish soda bread on the side.

16-oz. pkg. wide egg noodles,
   uncooked
1 lb. ground pork sausage

1 head cabbage, shredded
salt and pepper to taste

Cook noodles according to package instructions; drain. While noodles are cooking, brown sausage in a skillet over medium heat. Drain sausage and set aside, reserving some drippings in skillet. Add cabbage, salt and pepper to skillet; cook until cabbage is tender. Toss together cooked noodles, sausage and cabbage in a serving bowl. Makes 4 to 6 servings.

If a recipe calls for canned tomatoes, take advantage of Italian or Mexican style. They already have the seasonings added, so there are fewer ingredients for you to buy and measure!

Pasta in Tomato-Basil Sauce

Beth Schlieper
Lakewood, CO

*After tasting this scrumptious dish at a favorite Italian restaurant, my
husband and I came up with this very close recipe. I have been
making it ever since...that's nearly twenty years now!*

3 14-1/2 oz. cans diced
   tomatoes, partially drained
1 onion, diced
5 cloves garlic, minced
1/4 c. olive oil

3 T. dried basil
16-oz. pkg. angel hair pasta,
   uncooked
Garnish: grated Parmesan
   cheese

In a large saucepan over medium heat, combine all ingredients except
pasta and Parmesan cheese. Bring to a boil. Reduce heat to low; cover
and simmer for about 20 minutes, stirring occasionally. Meanwhile,
cook pasta according to package directions; drain. Serve sauce over
cooked pasta; sprinkle with cheese. Serves 6 to 8.

Extra cooked pasta doesn't need to go to waste. Toss with oil,
wrap tightly and refrigerate up to four days. To serve, place in
a metal colander, dip into boiling water for one minute
and drain...as good as fresh-cooked!

Pasta Pesto & Cherry Tomatoes

Barbara Bargdill
Gooseberry Patch

My cherry tomato plants produced a bumper crop this year! This is the perfect recipe to use fresh cherry tomatoes from your garden or from the farmers' market.

12-oz. pkg. rotini or fusilli
    pasta, uncooked
3 c. cherry tomatoes, quartered
salt to taste
1/4 c. basil pesto sauce

1-1/2 c. shredded mozzarella
    cheese
Garnish: shredded Romano
    cheese

Cook pasta according to package directions, just until tender. Drain, reserving one cup of cooking liquid. Return pasta to cooking pot. In a bowl, sprinkle tomatoes lightly with salt and toss with pesto. Add tomato mixture to hot pasta and toss; add some of reserved cooking liquid to moisten. Add mozzarella cheese; toss to combine. Sprinkle Romano cheese over each serving. Serves 4.

Some other yummy ways to enjoy pesto sauce...serve with grilled meat or baked fish. Stir into hot pasta dishes or vegetables. Add to sour cream or mayonnaise to make a dressing.

Pepper & Onion Brats

Lorrie Smith
Drummonds, TN

I first tried one of these sandwiches at a large outdoor flea market. Now I make them at home and they are always a big hit! With a side of coleslaw or potato salad, they're an easy dinner everyone enjoys.

1 T. canola oil
2 onions, chopped
2 green peppers, thinly sliced
6 smoked bratwurst sausages

salt and pepper to taste
6 hot dog buns, split
Garnish: mustard

Heat oil in a large skillet over medium heat. Add onions, peppers and bratwursts. Cover and cook about 5 minutes. Uncover; continue cooking until onions are translucent and golden. Add salt and pepper to taste. Place a brat and some of the onion mixture on each hot dog bun; top generously with mustard. Makes 6 servings.

Smoked sausages are a great choice for weeknight meals...just heat and serve. Different flavors like hickory-smoked or cheese-filled can really jazz up a recipe. Be sure to select fully-cooked sausages, not the uncooked kind.

5-Ingredient *Favorites*

Smoky Sausage Skillet

Carla Langston
Las Vegas, NV

One of my favorite go-to quick meals...it practically cooks itself!

14-oz. pkg. mini smoked turkey
   sausages
10-oz. pkg. sliced mushrooms
2 t. garlic, chopped

2 14-1/2 oz. cans cut green
   beans, drained
Optional: cooked rice

Spray a large skillet with non-stick vegetable spray. Brown sausages over medium heat. Add mushrooms and garlic. Cook, stirring occasionally, until mushrooms are tender. Add green beans; cook over low heat until heated through. Serve over cooked rice, if desired. Serves 6.

Set out all the fixin's for a baked potato bar for dinner tonight!
Let the kids choose their favorite toppers...a fun way
to serve a satisfying, simple meal.

Good Ol' Sloppy Joes

*Nancy Wysock
New Port Richey, FL*

I used to take these to work and everyone loved them. They're also much requested at church potlucks.

1 lb. ground beef chuck
1/2 c. onion, finely chopped
8-oz. can tomato sauce
2 T. honey
1/4 t. dry mustard

1/2 t. salt
1/4 t. pepper
4 hamburger buns or 8 slices
   bread

Brown beef in a skillet over medium heat; drain. Add onion; cook for 3 minutes. Stir in remaining ingredients except rolls or bread. Simmer for 5 minutes. Spoon onto buns or bread. Serves 4.

Mini Onion Burgers

*Mary Hall
Kentwood, MI*

Just add chips and sodas for a quick, fun meal almost anytime!

1 red onion, sliced
1 lb. lean ground beef
1/4 t. salt
1/8 t. pepper
12 to 15 small potato rolls, split

6 T. mayonnaise
2 T. Dijon mustard
1/2 to 1 t. cayenne pepper
Optional: mustard, catsup or
   mayonnaise

Preheat a flat-top grill pan over high heat. Add onion and cook until tender, about 10 minutes; remove to a bowl. In a separate bowl, mix beef, salt and pepper. Form into small patties, about 2 inches across. Add patties to grill pan; cook 3 to 4 minutes per side. For Special Sauce, mix mayonnaise, mustard and cayenne pepper in a small bowl. Serve patties on buns with grilled onion, Special Sauce and other toppings, if desired. Makes 12 to 15 servings.

5-Ingredient *Favorites*

All-In-One Bacon Cheeseburgers

*Beth Ann Richter
Canby, MN*

One day I had these ingredients on hand and decided to toss them together. My sister tweaked the recipe a little bit and they were even more delicious. Now they're a hit at all our family get-togethers!

1-1/2 lbs. lean ground beef
1-oz. pkg. ranch salad dressing
  mix
3-oz. jar bacon bits

8-oz. pkg. finely shredded
  Italian-blend cheese
6 hamburger buns, split

Place beef in a large bowl. Mix in remaining ingredients except buns, one at a time. Form into 6 patties. Grill over low heat, until burgers are lightly browned on one side. Turn and grill on other side. Burgers may also be cooked in a skillet over medium-low heat, covered, about 3 to 4 minutes per side. For either method, watch carefully to avoid burning. Serve on buns. Makes 6 servings.

Buttery, sweet corn on the cob is so delicious in the summertime...why not enjoy it more often? Place 3 tablespoons melted butter in a microwave-safe dish, add 4 husked ears of corn and roll to coat. Cover with plastic wrap and microwave on high for 6 to 8 minutes.

Mama's Halushki

Staci Prickett
Montezuma, GA

I grew up with this comfort food! It's one of my favorites. Halushki is usually a meatless side dish, but Mama always added meat to make it a meal. Garlic salt and cracked pepper really add flavor to this dish, so don't skimp on the seasonings!

8-oz. pkg. medium egg noodles, uncooked
1 lb. bacon or Kielbasa sausage, cut up, or ground beef
Optional: 2 to 4 T. butter, divided
1 head cabbage, cut up
1 onion, chopped
garlic salt and cracked pepper to taste

Cook noodles in salted water according to package directions; drain. Meanwhile, in a large skillet over medium heat, brown meat. If bacon is used, reserve drippings in skillet; otherwise, drain and add 2 tablespoons butter. Add cabbage and onion to skillet; cook for 5 to 10 minutes. Season to taste with garlic salt and cracked pepper. Reduce heat to low; cover and cook cabbage to desired tenderness. Stir in drained noodles during last 5 to 10 minutes of cooking. If desired, stir in remaining butter. Makes 8 servings.

Give noodles and pasta lots more flavor in a jiffy...just add a chicken or beef bouillon cube to the cooking water.

Spicy "Stuffed" Peppers

Loreen Brooks
Indianapolis, IN

A new twist on an old favorite. The New Orleans-style rice mix
gives it a very spicy bite that my family just loves!

1 lb. ground beef
1 onion, chopped
salt, pepper, garlic powder and
    onion powder to taste
2 8-oz. pkgs. dirty rice mix

14-1/2 oz. can stewed tomatoes,
    chopped
4-1/2 c. water
3 green peppers, halved

In a large skillet over medium heat, cook beef with onion. Drain; add
seasonings to taste. Add rice mixes, tomatoes with juice and water to
beef mixture; stir and bring to a boil. Place green peppers cut-side
down into beef mixture. Cover and cook over medium-low heat about
20 to 25 minutes, until liquid is absorbed and rice is tender. To serve,
spoon beef mixture onto dinner plates; top each with a green pepper
half. Makes 6 servings.

Keep a can of non-stick vegetable spray near the stove...quickly
spritz on a casserole dish or skillet for easy clean-up later.

Hamburg Gravy

Debbie Grywalski
Summerfield, OH

This old-fashioned recipe is my mother's favorite meal. It's really scrumptious over mashed potatoes!

1 lb. ground beef	4 t. beef bouillon granules
1/2 c. oil, divided	salt and pepper to taste
1/4 c. all-purpose flour	mashed potatoes
2 c. hot water	

In a skillet over medium heat, brown beef in 1/4 cup oil. Drain; remove beef from skillet and set aside. Add remaining oil and flour to skillet. Cook and stir for 2 minutes. In a small bowl, combine hot water and bouillon; stir until dissolved. Add bouillon mixture to skillet; cook and stir until thickened. Return beef to gravy in skillet. Add salt and pepper to taste. Serve over mashed potatoes. Serves 4.

A quick & easy seasoning mix is six parts salt to one part pepper. Keep it close to the stove in a large shaker...so handy when pan-frying pork chops, burgers or chicken.

Amish Goulash

Leticia Edington
Clinton, IN

Serve with a tossed salad and hot rolls for a satisfying meal prepared in less than thirty minutes!

5 to 8 potatoes, peeled and diced
10-oz. pkg. frozen peas
1 lb. ground beef
10-3/4 oz. can cream of celery
    soup

8-oz. pkg. favorite shredded
    cheese, divided

Place potatoes in a stockpot filled with boiling water. Cook over medium-high heat until potatoes are almost tender, about 15 minutes; add peas. Meanwhile, brown beef in a skillet over medium heat; drain. Add soup and cheese to beef, reserving some cheese for topping. Stir until well blended and cheese is melted. Drain potatoes and peas; add to beef mixture. Stir together; top with reserved cheese. Serves 6 to 8.

6:30
practice

Clip-type clothespins make such handy refrigerator clips...just glue a magnet on the back and they're ideal for holding appointment cards, newspaper clippings and the latest new recipes to try.

Tuna Pot Pie for Pennies

Judy Lange
Imperial, PA

Keep these ingredients on hand to bake up in a pinch!

6-1/2 oz. can tuna, drained
10-3/4 oz. can cream of
  mushroom soup

16-oz. can peas, drained
7-1/2 oz. tube refrigerated
  biscuits

Combine tuna, soup and peas in a bowl. Place in a greased
8"x8" baking pan. Arrange biscuits on top of tuna mixture. Bake,
uncovered, at 425 degrees for 15 minutes, or until hot and biscuits
are golden. Serves 2 to 3.

Tuna Pasta Dish

Helena Czanik
San Diego, CA

*I used to love eating this as a child. It's been a favorite with
the kids in the family for as long as I can remember.*

1 c. elbow or shell macaroni,
  uncooked
2.6-oz. pouch chunk light tuna,
  drained
1/2 c. favorite shredded cheese

5 T. mayonnaise-style salad
  dressing
5 T. catsup
salt and pepper to taste

Cook macaroni according to package directions; drain. In a
microwave-safe bowl, mix remaining ingredients together. Add
cooked macaroni to tuna mixture. Microwave on high for 30 to
60 seconds, until hot and bubbly. Serves 2, or one adult and 2 kids.

There's no need to be formal with one-dish dinners...set the dish
in the center of the dinner table and let everyone help themselves!

Mini Chicken Pot Pies

Amy Hunt
Traphill, NC

This is a speedy meal on a busy night. Just add some mashed potatoes,
a vegetable on the side and a simple dessert.

7-1/2 oz. tube refrigerated
    biscuits
1 c. cooked chicken, diced
10-3/4 oz. can cream of chicken
    soup

2/3 c. shredded sharp Cheddar
    cheese
salt and pepper to taste

Spray 8 to 10 muffin cups with non-stick vegetable spray. Place a
biscuit in each muffin cup; press down and 1/4 of the way up the
sides. In a bowl, combine remaining ingredients; stir until well
blended. Spoon chicken mixture into biscuit cups, filling about
3/4 full. Bake at 350 degrees for 10 to 15 minutes, until biscuits are
golden. Makes 4 to 5 servings, 2 pot pies each.

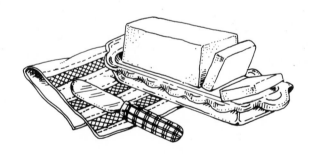

Whip up some savory herb butter. Blend 1/2 cup softened butter,
one tablespoon chopped fresh parsley, 1-1/2 teaspoons minced garlic,
one teaspoon Italian seasoning and a generous squirt of lemon
juice. Wrap well and refrigerate or freeze. To use, slice off a few pats
and thaw briefly...ready to jazz up hot rolls, mashed potatoes,
steamed veggies, scrambled eggs or even grilled steaks!

Busy-Day Lasagna

Meredith Martin
Austin, MN

This recipe is quick & easy when you just don't have time to spend all day in the kitchen. If you buy the ravioli on sale, this recipe is much more budget-friendly than traditional lasagna, too.

2 c. shredded mozzarella cheese
1 to 1-1/2 c. shredded Parmesan
   cheese
2 26-oz. jars favorite pasta
   sauce, divided

2 25-oz. pkgs. frozen sausage
   and cheese ravioli, divided
12-oz. pkg. frozen spinach,
   thawed and drained, divided

Combine cheeses in a bowl; set aside. Spread a layer of sauce in a lightly greased 13"x9" baking pan. Arrange a layer of ravioli on top of sauce. Spread a layer of spinach on top. Add a layer of cheese mixture, completely covering the spinach. Spoon some sauce over cheese. Repeat all of the layers, ending with a layer of cheese. Bake, uncovered, at 350 degrees for 20 to 25 minutes, until cheese is melted and sauce has reduced a little. Let stand 5 to 10 minutes before cutting into squares. Makes 8 to 12 servings.

Toss together salads for several days' meals so dinner is ready in a hurry. Store salad greens in a plastic zipping bag, tucking in a paper towel to absorb extra moisture and refrigerate. They'll stay crisp up to four days.

Tried & True Meatloaf

Lois Glines
Rogers, AR

I received this simple recipe from a 105-year-old lady I cared for. I have made this time and time again, and I promise it won't last long at your house. Yummy!

1 lb. ground beef
1 egg, beaten
13 saltine crackers, crushed

1/2 c. onion, chopped
1/2 t. salt
1/2 c. catsup, divided

In a bowl, combine beef, egg, cracker crumbs, onion, salt and 1/4 cup catsup. Mix well and place in an ungreased 9"x5" loaf pan. Spread remaining catsup on top. Bake, uncovered, at 350 degrees for 40 minutes, or until no longer pink. Serves 4.

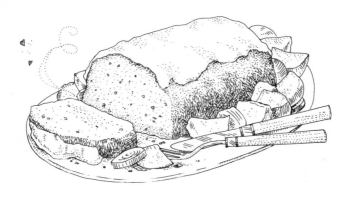

Cook once, eat twice! Make a double batch of meatloaf, meatballs or taco beef, then freeze half. On a busy night, how wonderful to simply pull dinner from the freezer, reheat and serve.

Melinda's Mexican Manicotti

Melinda Magness
Hodgen, OK

This is a recipe that I changed to fit my tastes. Even my picky boys love it! We like to have beans and rice with it.

8-oz. pkg. manicotti shells,
   uncooked
1 lb. lean ground beef
1-1/4 oz. pkg. taco seasoning
   mix

3/4 c. water
16-oz. jar mild or hot picante
   sauce
8-oz. pkg. shredded
   Mexican-blend cheese

Cook pasta shells according to package directions; drain. While shells are cooking, brown beef in a skillet over medium heat; drain. Stir in taco seasoning mix and water; reduce heat and simmer for 5 minutes. With a small spoon, fill cooked shells with beef mixture. Arrange shells in a lightly greased 13"x9" baking pan. Spoon picante sauce over top; sprinkle with cheese. Bake, uncovered, at 350 degrees for 30 minutes, or until hot and bubbly. Serves 4.

Toss together a cool, easy side for 6...corn and tomato salad. Combine a drained can of corn, a drained can of diced tomatoes with sweet onions, 3 sliced green onions and 1/4 cup chopped fresh parsley or cilantro. Add 1/3 cup lime juice, 1/3 cup seasoned rice vinegar and salt to taste. Pop in the fridge and chill until dinnertime.

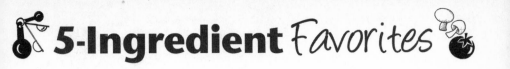

5-Ingredient *Favorites*

Chicken Chilaquiles

Sharon Gutierrez
Escondido, CA

I like to figure out shortcuts to make recipes quick & easy. I combined a few different recipes to make this extremely yummy dinner. Try it...I think you'll agree!

1/2 c. oil
10 corn tortillas, cut into
   1/2-inch strips
Optional: salt to taste
1 c. shredded mozzarella cheese

1 c. shredded Cheddar cheese
2 c. cooked chicken, shredded
28-oz. can mild chile verde
   sauce, divided

Heat oil in a skillet over medium heat, until hot. Cook tortilla strips, a few at a time, just until crispy. Drain tortilla strips on paper towels; sprinkle with salt, if desired. Mix cheeses in a bowl; set aside. Spray a 13"x9" baking pan with non-stick vegetable spray. Layer half of the tortilla strips in pan; top with chicken, one cup sauce and one cup cheese mixture. Press layers gently down into pan. Repeat layering with remaining tortilla strips, sauce and cheese. Bake, uncovered, at 350 degrees for about 30 minutes, or until cheese is melted and golden. Makes 6 to 8 servings.

Put your pizza cutter to work full-time. It's perfect for cutting tortillas into strips and slicing cheesy quesadillas into wedges...you're sure to discover other uses!

Hillary's Pretzel Chicken

Hillary Pence
Grottoes, VA

I'm always looking for quick dinner ideas for when I get home after a hard day's work. This recipe is so easy and my husband enjoys it too. Butter pretzels are tasty, but use whatever you have on hand!

1-1/2 c. pretzels
1/4 c. butter, melted
4 to 6 boneless, skinless
   chicken breasts

Garnish: honey mustard or
   other favorite mustard

Place pretzels in a plastic zipping bag; seal. With a mallet, crush finely. Place melted butter in a shallow bowl. Dip chicken into butter; add to crushed pretzels in zipping bag and coat well. Place chicken in a greased 13"x9" baking pan. Bake, uncovered, at 350 degrees for about 20 to 25 minutes, until chicken juices run clear. Serve with mustard for dipping. Makes 4 to 6 servings.

Parmesan-Crusted Chicken

Kimberly Hancock
Murrieta, CA

This recipe is so easy, I can make it with my eyes closed...terrific for a busy weeknight. Serve on a bed of spaghetti with marinara sauce

1/2 c. mayonnaise
1/4 c. grated Parmesan cheese
1/4 c. Italian-seasoned dry
   bread crumbs

4 boneless, skinless chicken
   breasts

Combine mayonnaise and cheese. Spread mixture over chicken; sprinkle with bread crumbs. Arrange in a lightly greased 13"x9" baking pan. Bake, uncovered, at 425 degrees for 20 minutes, or until chicken juices run clear. Serves 4.

Crispy Corn Flake Chicken

Dana Cunningham
Lafayette, LA

My family loves take-out chicken by the bucket, but this oven-fried version is healthier and just as yummy. Well, except for the time that I used sugar-frosted cereal by mistake...I won't do that again!

8 chicken drumsticks and/or
   thighs
salt and pepper to taste
1 egg, beaten
1 T. water

2 c. corn flake cereal, crushed
1 T. olive oil
1 t. salt
Optional: 1/2 t. cayenne pepper

Remove skin from chicken; discard. Sprinkle chicken generously with salt and pepper. In a small bowl, whisk egg with water. In a shallow bowl, mix crushed cereal, oil, salt and cayenne pepper, if desired. Dip chicken into egg mixture; coat with cereal mixture, pressing it on well. Arrange chicken on a greased 15"x10" jelly-roll pan. Bake, uncovered, at 400 degrees until crisp, golden and chicken juices run clear, about 30 minutes. Makes 8 servings.

Need a quick after-school snack to tide the kids over until dinnertime? Hand out little bags of crunchy snacks...just toss together bite-size cereal squares, raisins or dried cranberries and a few chocolate-covered candies.

Hearty Potato Puff Bake

Amy Wade
Stephenville, TX

This dish was a favorite while I was working as a paramedic. It's speedy to fix and easy to double so that everyone on shift at the station can enjoy a tasty hot meal. Serve as soon as it's ready...you never know when you will get called away!

2 lbs. lean ground beef
1 c. onion, chopped
salt and pepper to taste
10-3/4 oz. can cream of
   mushroom soup

4 c. shredded Cheddar cheese,
   divided
32-oz. pkg. frozen potato puffs

In a large skillet over medium heat, brown beef and onion; drain. Season with salt and pepper; stir in soup and 2 cups cheese. Add beef mixture to a 13"x9" baking pan sprayed with non-stick vegetable spray. Arrange potato puffs on top. Bake, uncovered, at 375 degrees for 25 minutes, until potato puffs are golden. Top with remaining cheese. Bake, uncovered, for an additional 10 minutes, until cheese melts. Serves 8 to 10.

Speed up prep time on ground beef recipes! Brown several
pounds of beef, adding onions and green peppers if you like.
Divide into one-pound portions in large plastic freezer bags
and flatten to freeze. Thaw overnight in the fridge,
or even in the microwave anytime it's needed.

Family Love Spaghetti Pie

Ilene Breton
Winchendon, MA

This simple get-together dish has been in our family for years. One of our family members would make four or five casseroles and we would all gather at their house to eat and have fun. The flavor is even better if you use a mixture of cheeses!

16-oz. pkg. spaghetti, uncooked
2 to 3 28-oz. cans whole
    tomatoes, drained and sliced

4 c. shredded white Cheddar
    cheese

Cook spaghetti according to package directions; drain. In a greased 3-quart casserole dish, layer half of spaghetti, half of tomatoes and half of cheese. Repeat layering, ending with cheese on top. Bake, uncovered, at 350 degrees for 30 to 45 minutes, until bubbly and heated through. Serves 6.

For a side dish that practically cooks itself, fill aluminum foil packets with sliced fresh veggies. Top with seasoning salt and two ice cubes; seal. Bake at 450 degrees for 20 to 25 minutes, or alongside a casserole at 350 degrees for a little longer. Delicious!

Quick Chicken Parmesan

Amy Blanchard
Clawson, MI

So easy and so good! If you prefer, use cooked boneless chicken breasts instead of the breaded patties.

16-oz. pkg. spaghetti or other pasta, uncooked
24-oz. jar favorite pasta sauce, divided
1 c. shredded mozzarella cheese, divided

4 to 6 frozen breaded chicken patties
1/4 c. grated Parmesan cheese

Cook pasta according to package directions; drain. In a bowl, toss cooked pasta with 2/3 of sauce. Spread evenly into a 13"x9" baking pan sprayed with non-stick vegetable spray. Sprinkle with 1/2 cup mozzarella cheese; arrange frozen chicken patties on top. Spoon remaining sauce over all; sprinkle with remaining mozzarella and Parmesan cheeses. Cover with aluminum foil. Bake at 350 degrees for 20 to 30 minutes, until heated through. Serve each chicken patty over a portion of pasta. Makes 4 to 6 servings.

Ready, set, cook! If the oven will be used, turn it on right away to preheat. When pasta is on the menu, put a big pot of water on the stove as soon as you get home. Dinner will be ready in a jiffy!

Grammy's Chicken à la King

Elizabeth Cerri
Stephens City, VA

This is a mainstay dish that my grandmother would whip up on snowy days in Connecticut. We'd come in from sled riding, chilled to the bone. Grammy knew just how to warm us up...with her quick Chicken à la King over biscuits or rice. Mmm!

1 T. oil
4 boneless, skinless chicken breasts, cut into 1-inch cubes
2 10-3/4 oz. cans cream of chicken soup

1/2 c. milk
2 15-oz. cans mixed vegetables, drained
salt and pepper to taste
4 biscuits or cooked rice

In a large skillet over medium heat, heat oil. Add chicken and sauté until no longer pink, about 5 minutes. In a bowl, whisk together soup and milk until smooth. Stir in vegetables. Spoon soup mixture over chicken in skillet. Reduce heat to low. Cover and simmer for about 10 minutes, until heated through. Add salt and pepper to taste. Serve over split biscuits or rice. Serves 4.

Keep cooking oil in a glass bottle with a pouring spout.
This makes it easy to drizzle oil just where it's needed,
with no waste and no mess...clever!

Brandy's Chicken on a Stick

Brandy Golden
Baden, PA

Whenever I make these chicken sticks, the kids go crazy! My family requests them for every cookout. Yummy!

4 boneless, skinless chicken
   breasts
1/4 c. soy sauce
1/4 c. brown sugar, packed

2 T. honey
1 t. ground ginger
6 to 8 wooden skewers, soaked
   in water

Cut each chicken breast lengthwise into 4 strips. Pound strips until thin; place in a large plastic zipping bag. Mix remaining ingredients in a bowl; add half of sauce mixture to chicken in bag. Refrigerate chicken for 2 hours to overnight. Refrigerate remaining sauce mixture in a separate container for basting. Drain chicken; discard bag and marinade. Thread chicken strips onto skewers. Grill over medium heat for about 3 minutes on each side, basting with reserved sauce mixture. Makes 6 to 8 servings.

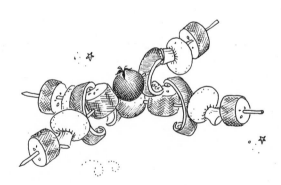

Just for fun, serve fresh veggies on sticks, too...kids love it!
Thread bite-size veggies like cherry tomatoes, whole mushrooms,
yellow pepper squares and baby carrots onto skewers.
Serve with ranch salad dressing for tasty dipping.

🥄 5-Ingredient *Favorites* 🍅

Honey-Mustard Grilled Chicken

Diana Chaney
Olathe, KS

So simple, yet so tasty! If you prefer to use boneless, skinless chicken breasts, cut large pieces in half.

2/3 c. Dijon mustard
1/2 c. honey
1/4 c. mayonnaise

2 t. red steak sauce
8 boneless, skinless chicken
  thighs

In a shallow bowl, whisk together all ingredients except chicken. Set aside 1/3 of mustard mixture for basting. Coat chicken in remaining mustard mixture. Grill chicken over medium heat for 18 to 20 minutes, turning occasionally, until chicken juices run clear. Brush occasionally with reserved mustard mixture during the last 10 minutes. Makes 8 servings.

Don't toss that almost-empty Dijon mustard jar! Use it to mix up a zesty salad dressing. Pour 3 tablespoons olive oil, 2 tablespoons cider vinegar and a clove of minced garlic into the jar, replace the lid and shake well. Add salt and pepper to taste. Drizzle over mixed greens...so refreshing.

Hot Dog "Cupcakes"

Bethany Newton
Centreville, VA

These taste just like corn dogs...kids love 'em! My girls gave this recipe its name. Dip them in catsup...yummy!

8-1/2 oz. pkg. corn muffin mix
1/3 c. water
1 egg, beaten
1/4 c. shredded Cheddar cheese

4 to 6 hot dogs, cut into
   bite-size pieces
Garnish: catsup

In a bowl, stir together muffin mix, water and egg. Add cheese and hot dogs; blend together. Fill paper-lined muffin cups 2/3 full. Bake at 400 degrees for 15 to 20 minutes, until golden. Serve with catsup. Makes 6 servings.

Chili Dog Pizzas

Jill Duvendack
Pioneer, OH

My grandchildren love making and eating these pizzas...soooo easy. This recipe serves Grandpa, Grandma, two grandkids and possibly Mom, if she gets here before it's gone!

2 12-inch ready-to-bake
   pizza crusts
1 to 2 15-oz. cans chili without
   beans

6 to 8 hot dogs, sliced
8-oz. pkg. shredded Cheddar-
   Monterey Jack cheese, or
   more to taste

Place crusts on ungreased pizza pans. Top each crust with half of the chili; spread to cover. Arrange hot dogs over chili; top with cheese. Bake according to crust package directions, until golden and cheese has melted. Serves 4 to 6.

Fill the sink with hot soapy water when you start dinner and just toss in pans and utensils as they're used...clean-up will be a breeze.

5-Ingredient *Favorites*

Nan's Stuffed Hot Dogs

Nancy Rossman
Port Richey, FL

*This simple recipe was passed down to me from my mother. We love
these delicious dogs with a side of French fries or home fries. I fix two
per person, but hearty eaters may want more!*

16-oz. pkg. bun-length hot dogs
16-oz. can baked beans
8 long thin slices kosher dill
   pickle

6 slices American cheese,
   cut into thirds
8 slices bacon

Slice hot dogs lengthwise, but not all the way through. Spoon a
tablespoonful of beans into each hot dog. Top with one pickle slice
and 2 pieces of cheese; wrap hot dog in a bacon slice. Place on a
baking sheet sprayed with non-stick vegetable spray. Bake, uncovered,
at 350 degrees for 30 minutes, or until bacon is crisp on top. Makes
8 servings.

White paper coffee filters make tidy toss-away holders
for hot dog buns, sandwich wraps or tacos.

Poor Man's Lobster

Linda Stone
Smithville, TN

For the mildest tasting, most tender monkfish, choose lighter colored fillets. If you like, use olive oil for baking, then butter for dipping.

1-1/2 lbs. monkfish fillets
1 c. butter, melted and divided
salt, pepper and paprika to taste

lemon zest to taste
Garnish: lemon slices, fresh
  parsley sprigs

Arrange fish fillets in a lightly greased shallow 13"x9" baking pan. Drizzle half of melted butter over fish; sprinkle with seasonings to taste. Add a little lemon zest to remaining butter; set aside and keep warm. Bake fish, uncovered, at 375 degrees for 15 to 25 minutes, until fish flakes easily with a fork. Garnish as desired; serve with warm lemon butter for dipping. Makes 4 servings.

Crisp coleslaw pairs well with fish dishes. Perk up your favorite coleslaw with some mandarin oranges or pineapple tidbits for a delicious change.

Mom's Salmon Crisps

Andrea Ford
Montfort, WI

This was one of my mom's recipes. A quick & easy supper.

16-oz. can salmon, drained and
    flaked
1 egg, beaten
2 T. milk
1/2 t. salt

1/4 t. pepper
1/2 c. fine saltine cracker
    crumbs
1/4 c. butter, melted

In a bowl, mix salmon, egg, milk, salt and pepper. Form into 8 to 9 oblong rolls. Roll each in cracker crumbs. Place rolls in a greased shallow 13"x9" baking pan; drizzle with butter. Bake, uncovered, at 400 degrees for 25 to 30 minutes. Serves 4.

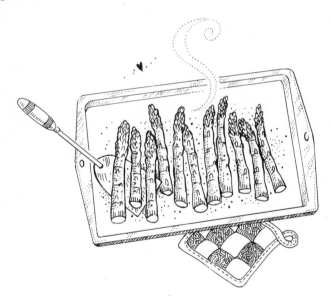

Roasted fresh asparagus is simply delicious...simple to fix too.
Arrange spears on a baking sheet and sprinkle with olive oil and
garlic salt. Bake at 425 degrees for 10 to 15 minutes. Serve warm
or at room temperature.

Easy Garlic Chicken

Theresa Wehmeyer
Rosebud, MO

My family loves this chicken, and so do I! The short list of ingredients is easy to remember when I'm at the grocery store wondering what to make for dinner.

4 boneless, skinless chicken
  breasts
1/3 c. mayonnaise
1/4 c. grated Parmesan cheese

3 to 4 T. savory herb & garlic
  soup mix
2 T. dry bread crumbs

Place chicken in a greased 11"x7" baking pan. In a small bowl, combine mayonnaise, Parmesan cheese and soup mix. Spread chicken with mayonnaise mixture; sprinkle with bread crumbs. Bake, uncovered, at 400 degrees for 20 to 25 minutes, until chicken juices run clear when pierced. Makes 4 servings.

Creamy Olive-Stuffed Chicken

Renae Scheiderer
Beallsville, OH

This is a recipe that I've recently tried. It's good for my diabetic diet...I've adjusted it a bit so that the whole family enjoys it!

4 boneless, skinless chicken
  breasts
1/2 c. cream cheese, softened
2-1/4 oz. can sliced black olives,
  drained

1/8 t. dried oregano
1/8 t. pepper
1/2 c. seasoned dry bread
  crumbs
1 T. olive oil

Flatten chicken breasts to 1/4-inch thickness. In a bowl, combine cream cheese, olives, oregano and pepper. Spoon 2 tablespoons of mixture down the center of each chicken breast. Fold chicken over filling; secure with toothpicks, if desired, and roll in bread crumbs. In a large, ovenproof skillet over medium heat, cook chicken in oil until golden. Place skillet in oven. Bake, uncovered, at 350 degrees for 20 to 25 minutes, until chicken juices run clear. Makes 4 servings.

One-Dish
Dinners

Creole Pork Chops & Rice

Phyllis Covington
Guthrie, KY

This flavorful one-pot meal really smells amazing as it cooks...even the leftovers taste wonderful! It's yummy made with boneless, skinless chicken breasts instead of pork chops too.

4 pork chops	1 c. long-cooking rice, uncooked
1 T. oil	29-oz. can tomato sauce
1 c. onion, diced	15-oz. can diced tomatoes
1 c. celery, diced	salt and pepper to taste

In a skillet over medium heat, cook pork chops in oil until golden but not cooked through. Add onion, celery and uncooked rice; stir in remaining ingredients. Reduce heat to low. Cover and simmer until rice is tender, about 15 to 20 minutes, adding more water as needed to prevent drying out. Makes 4 servings.

Homemade applesauce goes so well with pork chops...why not make some while dinner is cooking? Peel, core and chop four tart apples. Combine with 1/4 cup water, 2 teaspoons brown sugar and 1/8 teaspoon cinnamon in a microwave-safe bowl. Cover and microwave on high for 8 to 10 minutes. Mash apples with a potato masher and serve warm, dusted with a little more cinnamon.

Stir-Fried Pork & Noodles

Jill Ross
Gooseberry Patch

Stir-fries are my easy answer to dinner in a hurry. They're so adaptable too...you can use boneless chicken, beef or even portabella mushrooms instead of pork.

5 c. water, divided
2 3-oz. pkgs. Oriental-flavor
  ramen noodles, divided
2 t. oil, divided
16-oz. pkg. frozen stir-fry
  vegetables, thawed

1/2 c. onion, sliced
3 cloves garlic, minced
3/4 lb. boneless pork chops,
  cut into strips
1 T. cornstarch
Optional: soy sauce

In a saucepan over high heat, bring 4 cups water to a boil. Add noodles; set aside seasoning packets. Boil noodles for 3 minutes; drain. Meanwhile, add one teaspoon oil to a large skillet over medium-high heat. Add vegetables, onion and garlic to skillet. Cook and stir until crisp-tender, about 4 minutes. Set vegetable mixture aside in a bowl. Add pork and remaining oil to skillet. Cook and stir just until pork is cooked through. Remove pork to bowl with vegetables. Combine remaining water, reserved seasoning packets and cornstarch in skillet. Stir until simmering and well-blended. Cook for one minute, or until slightly thickened. Add noodles; toss to coat. Add pork and vegetables. Cook and stir gently over low heat until warmed through. Serve with soy sauce, if desired. Makes 4 servings.

Use a long-handled wooden spatula when stir-frying to lift and turn the food easily without scratching the pan.

Chicken & Mushroom Risotto

*Judy Young
Plano, TX*

*I brought this recipe with me from England. It is simple
to make but oh-so good!*

1 c. long-cooking rice, uncooked
2 T. onion, minced
1/4 c. butter, divided
2 c. chicken broth
1/4 lb. sliced mushrooms

1/2 t. salt
1/8 t. paprika
1 c. cooked chicken, diced
1/2 c. shredded sharp Cheddar
   cheese

In a large saucepan over medium heat, combine rice, onion and
one tablespoon butter. Sauté for one to 3 minutes; stir in broth. Cook,
covered, over low heat for 30 minutes. While rice is cooking, sauté
mushrooms in remaining butter in a separate saucepan. When rice is
tender, stir in mushrooms and remaining ingredients. Cook an
additional 5 minutes, until heated through. Serves 4.

Cook up a big pot of chicken to freeze for later. For juicy, flavorful
chicken, cover with water and simmer gently until cooked through,
then turn off the heat and let the chicken cool in its own broth.
Shred or cube chicken, wrap well in recipe-size portions and freeze.

Deb's Chicken Florentine

Deb Eaton
Mesa, AZ

My husband loves Italian food! When a local restaurant closed, he was sad that he couldn't get his favorite dish anymore, so I recreated it for him at home. You can substitute frozen spinach, canned mushrooms or leftover rotisserie chicken. Serve with garlic bread sticks hot from the oven to sop up all the delicious juices!

16-oz. pkg. linguine pasta, uncooked
2 T. olive oil
3 cloves garlic, minced
4 boneless, skinless chicken breasts, thinly sliced
1-1/4 c. fat-free zesty Italian salad dressing, divided

8 sun-dried tomatoes, chopped
8-oz. pkg. sliced mushrooms
5-oz. pkg. baby spinach
cracked pepper to taste
Optional: grated Parmesan cheese, chopped fresh flat-leaf parsley

Cook pasta according to package directions; drain. While pasta is cooking, warm oil in a skillet over medium heat. Add garlic and cook 2 minutes. Add chicken; cook until no longer pink. Drizzle chicken with one cup salad dressing. Stir in tomatoes and mushrooms; cover skillet and simmer until mushrooms are softened. Add spinach; cover skillet again. Cook another 2 to 3 minutes, just until spinach is wilted; stir and sprinkle with pepper. Toss cooked linguine with remaining salad dressing. Serve chicken and vegetables over linguine, garnished as desired. Makes 6 servings.

Good china and candles aren't just for the holidays or special celebrations...use them to brighten everyday family meals!

Inside-Out Cabbage Rolls

Joyceann Dreibelbis
Wooster, OH

A low-fat, one-dish meal that gives you that down-home feel...and it's ready to serve in no time!

1 lb. ground beef
1 onion, chopped
1 green pepper, chopped
10-oz. can diced tomatoes and
   green chiles

1 head cabbage, chopped
1 c. beef broth
8-oz. can pizza sauce
1 c. cooked brown rice
1/2 c. shredded Cheddar cheese

In a Dutch oven over medium heat, cook beef, onion and green pepper until beef is no longer pink; drain. Stir in tomatoes, cabbage, broth and pizza sauce. Bring to a boil; reduce heat to low. Cover and simmer for 20 to 25 minutes, until cabbage is tender, stirring occasionally. Stir in rice; heat through. Remove from heat. Sprinkle with cheese; cover and let stand until cheese is melted. Serves 6.

Deviled Hamburgers

Lynn Knepp
Montgomery, IN

These yummy burgers marinate all day! This recipe came from one of my beauty salon customers who passed away over twenty-five years ago. Whenever I get out this recipe card and see her name written on it, I think of her, and that makes it extra special.

1 lb. ground beef
2 T. catsup
1 T. onion, chopped
2 t. mustard

1 t. red steak sauce
1 t. seasoned salt
1/2 t. pepper
4 hamburger buns, split

In the morning, mix together all ingredients except buns; form into 4 patties. Cover and refrigerate until evening. Cook as you prefer by frying in a skillet, or grilling on a countertop grill or an outdoor grill. Serve burgers on buns. Makes 4 servings.

Hamburger-Green Bean Skillet

Ann Smith
Columbus, OH

*This dish started with ready items from my pantry. It has
turned into easy, quick comfort food for my family!*

1 lb. ground beef
6.2-oz. pkg. fried rice-flavored
   rice vermicelli mix
2 c. water

1 T. Worcestershire sauce
1 to 2 14-1/2 oz. cans green
   beans, drained

Brown beef in a large skillet over medium heat; drain. When beef is
nearly done, stir in rice vermicelli mix. Cook, stirring frequently, until
rice turns light golden. Add remaining ingredients; bring to a boil.
Reduce heat; cover and simmer for 15 minutes. Serves 6.

Keep shopping simple...have a shopping list that includes all the
ingredients you use often, plus a few blank lines for special items.

Jackie's Quick Stir-Fry

Jackie Antweiler
Evergreen, CO

This is my version of a speedy stir-fry. Sometimes I use two kinds of meats or any extra veggies I have in the fridge for a tasty new meal made with leftovers.

16-oz. pkg. shredded broccoli-
   carrot or coleslaw mix
4 T. oil, divided
1 c. cooked ham, pork, chicken
   or shrimp, chopped or sliced
3 T. rice vinegar
3 T. soy sauce

3 T. sugar
salt and pepper to taste
3-oz. pkg. chicken-flavored
   ramen noodles
2-oz. pkg. slivered almonds
3 T. sesame seed

In a large skillet over medium-high heat, cook and stir shredded vegetables in 2 tablespoons oil. Add meat to skillet. In a small bowl, mix remaining oil, vinegar, soy sauce, sugar, salt, pepper and seasoning packet from ramen noodle package. Add oil mixture to skillet; stir well. Add almonds and sesame seed. Crush ramen noodles and add to skillet; simmer until noodles are soft, 3 to 4 minutes. Makes 4 servings.

Slice stir-fry meat and veggies into equal-size pieces...they'll all be cooked to perfection at the same time.

Mushroom Fried Rice

Jamie Courchesne
Alberta, Canada

*My Aunt Merle often serves this dish when we're invited
for supper at her house...we enjoy it very much!*

2 to 3 t. oil
1 c. sliced mushrooms
1 onion, chopped
1 c. cooked chicken, turkey
    or ham, diced
seasoned salt and pepper
    to taste

2 c. instant rice, uncooked
1/2 c. peas, corn or mixed
    vegetables
10-1/2 oz. can beef broth
1-1/4 c. water
1 t. soy sauce
1/2 t. dried parsley

In a large skillet, heat oil over medium heat. Add mushrooms, onion, meat, salt and pepper. Cook, stirring often, until mushrooms and onion are tender. Add uncooked rice and vegetables; cook and stir for 2 to 3 minutes. Add remaining ingredients. Cover and simmer over low heat for about 10 minutes, until rice is tender and liquid is absorbed. Serves 4.

Turn leftovers into plan-overs! When you create the week's menu, plan two meals that use some of the same ingredients. Extra baked chicken can become shredded chicken sandwiches another night...extra taco beef can be stirred into a pot of chili. The possibilities are endless and real time-savers.

Virgil's Veggie Fettuccine

*Jodi Spires
Centerville, OH*

My dad knew how to cook only a few things, but they were extraordinary! He has been gone for several years now...when our family sits down to this homemade meal, it's as if he is still right there with us, smiling.

2 16-oz. pkgs. fettuccine pasta, uncooked
1-1/2 c. half-and-half
2 t. garlic salt or powder
8 c. broccoli, cut into bite-sized pieces
1 head cauliflower, cut into bite-sized pieces
8-oz. pkg. sliced mushrooms
salt and pepper to taste
2 to 3 c. grated Parmesan cheese

Cook pasta according to package directions; drain. While pasta is cooking, combine half-and-half and garlic salt or powder in an extra-large Dutch oven. Heat over medium heat just until boiling. Add broccoli, cauliflower and mushrooms; stir to moisten. Season with additional garlic salt or powder, if desired, and salt and pepper. Cook over medium heat until vegetables are crisp-tender, stirring frequently; vegetables will cook down. Add cooked pasta; stir until everything is combined and heated through. Gradually add Parmesan cheese; stir until melted. Serve immediately. Makes 8 to 10 servings.

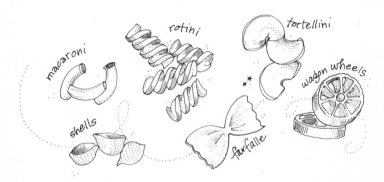

When a recipe calls for pasta, there are lots of shapes to choose from at the grocery store...why not experiment? Try using corkscrews, shells, bowties and rainbow pasta just for fun!

Adam's Vegetable Pasta

Susan Curtis
Glen Gardner, NJ

My sister's boyfriend, a professional chef, created this dish when they visited my husband and me in 1985, when we were first married. I've made this budget-friendly recipe ever since. I like it because it's meatless and low-fat, my husband likes the meaty flavor of the portabella mushrooms and the kids like it because there's always a vegetable they can pick out and refuse to eat!

16-oz. pkg. rotelle pasta, uncooked
2 to 4 T. olive oil
1 stalk celery, sliced
4 cloves garlic, sliced
1 sweet Italian frying pepper or cubanelle, cut into thin strips
1 zucchini, cut into thin strips
1 to 2 portabella mushrooms, sliced
28-oz. can diced tomatoes
1 T. sugar
1 T. cider vinegar
Optional: 1/2 to 1 t. lemon juice

Cook pasta according to package directions; drain. Meanwhile, add oil to a large skillet over low heat. Sauté celery in oil until soft. Add garlic; sauté about 3 minutes. Increase heat to medium. Add pepper, zucchini and mushrooms; sauté until soft. Add undrained tomatoes; bring to a simmer. Stir in remaining ingredients. Simmer until vegetables are tender. Serve vegetable mixture over cooked pasta. Makes 4 servings.

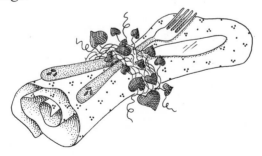

Whether dinner is casual, served in the kitchen, or a little more formal at the dining table, be sure to add simple, special touches...colorful napkins tied in a knot or perky blossoms tucked into a canning jar make mealtime more fun!

Chicken Noodle Bowl

Marla Caldwell
Forest, IN

This is a great fast-fix midweek meal! It takes just thirty minutes total cooking time.

8-oz. pkg. linguine pasta, uncooked
3 c. frozen broccoli cuts
2 carrots, peeled and sliced
2 t. oil
1 lb. boneless, skinless chicken breasts, cut into strips

1/2 c. zesty Italian salad dressing
1/3 c. teriyaki sauce
1 t. ground ginger

Cook pasta as package directs; add broccoli and carrots to the cooking water for last 2 minutes of cooking time. Drain pasta mixture. Meanwhile, heat oil in a large skillet over medium heat. Add chicken; cook until golden on all sides, stirring occasionally. Stir in remaining ingredients; cook until sauce thickens, stirring occasionally. Add pasta mixture to skillet. Stir until coated with sauce. Serve in individual bowls. Makes 4 servings.

Protect your favorite cookbook from cooking spatters...simply slip it inside a gallon-size plastic zipping bag.

Tomato & Chicken Penne

Stefanie St. Pierre
South Dennis, MA

This is a wonderfully hearty dish that's easy to prepare.

16-oz. pkg. penne pasta,
   uncooked
1/4 c. olive oil
1 t. garlic, chopped
28-oz. can diced tomatoes,
   drained
1/2 c. fresh basil, chopped, or
   1 t. dried basil

2 lbs. boneless, skinless chicken
   breasts, cooked and cubed
8-oz. pkg. shredded mozzarella
   cheese
salt and pepper to taste

Cook pasta according to package directions; drain. Meanwhile, heat oil in a skillet over medium heat. Add garlic; sauté for one minute. Stir in tomatoes and basil; continue cooking for 2 minutes. Add chicken to skillet. Simmer for about 5 minutes, until heated through. Transfer mixture in skillet to a large serving bowl; toss with pasta and cheese. Season with salt and pepper. Makes 6 to 8 servings.

After you unpack groceries, take just a little time to prep ingredients and place them in plastic zipping bags...wash and chop fruits and vegetables and place meats in marinades. Weeknight dinners will be so much easier.

Spanish Rice & Beef

Sue Hogarth
Lancaster, CA

This recipe is perfect when you need to get dinner on the table in a hurry, after working all day and shuttling the kids to their after-school activities. Warm up some dinner rolls...dinner is served!

1 lb. ground beef
14-1/2 oz. can stewed tomatoes
10-oz. pkg. frozen corn or
    mixed vegetables
1 c. water
1/2 t. dried oregano

1/2 t. chili powder
1/4 t. garlic powder
1/2 t. salt
1/8 t. pepper
1-1/2 c. instant rice, uncooked

Brown beef in a large skillet over medium heat; drain. Add undrained tomatoes, frozen corn or vegetables, water and seasonings. Bring to a boil; boil about 2 minutes, or until vegetables are tender. Stir in uncooked rice. Cover; remove from heat and let stand about 5 minutes. Fluff rice with a fork before serving. Makes 4 to 6 servings.

Make your own seasoning mixes! If you have a favorite busy-day recipe that calls for lots of different herbs or spices, measure them out into several small plastic zipping bags and label. Later, when time is short, just tip a bag into the cooking pot.

Texas Hash

Sharlene Casteel
Fort Mitchell, AL

I got this recipe from someone at church many years ago and it is still a family favorite...so easy! Add a side salad and dinner is ready in a jiffy.

1 lb. ground beef
1 onion, diced
1/2 red or green pepper, diced
1 c. long-cooking rice, uncooked
14-1/2 oz. can diced tomatoes

3 c. water
2 t. chili powder
1 t. paprika
salt and pepper to taste

In a skillet over medium heat, brown beef with onion and red or green pepper; drain. Stir in uncooked rice and remaining ingredients. Cover and simmer over low heat for about 25 minutes, until water is absorbed and rice is tender. Makes 4 to 6 servings.

Breakfast foods are so warm and comforting...try 'em for dinner as a special treat! Scrambled eggs and toast or pancakes and bacon are easy to stir up in minutes. Or assemble a family-favorite breakfast casserole in the morning and pop it in the oven at dinnertime.

Sweet-and-Sour Beef Bits

Tammie Douglas
Ossian, IN

My mom is usually a "dump" cook, making many dishes from memory, so I was surprised when she gave me this recipe with actual measurements. She measures with an old plastic scoop she's had for forty years. That old scoop has all the right measurements when it's in her hands, though, because everything she makes turns out perfect!

2 lbs. beef round steak, cut into
    1-1/2 inch cubes
4-oz. can sliced mushrooms,
    drained
3 T. butter
1/4 c. all-purpose flour
1 c. water
1/4 c. lemon juice

2 T. cider vinegar
1-1/2 t. dry mustard
2/3 c. brown sugar, packed
1.35-oz. pkg. onion soup mix
8-oz. can sliced water chestnuts,
    drained
chow mein noodles or
    cooked rice

In a large skillet over medium heat, brown beef and mushrooms in butter. Drain; transfer beef mixture to a bowl and set aside. Add flour, water, lemon juice and vinegar to skillet; cook and stir until golden. Add mustard, brown sugar, soup mix and water chestnuts; bring to a boil. Return beef mixture to skillet; reduce heat to low. Simmer, covered, for 30 minutes. Serve over chow mein noodles or cooked rice. Makes 6 to 8 servings.

Let the kids plan the family dinner once a week. Younger children can practice basic cooking skills, while older kids and teens might enjoy choosing and preparing their favorite Mexican or Italian meals.

Cajun Skillet Rice

Janine Tinklenberg
Redford, MI

I adapted this hearty recipe from one that my mom gave me.

1 T. olive oil
1 c. onion, chopped
1 c. green pepper, chopped
1 c. red pepper, chopped
1 lb. Kielbasa sausage, sliced
2 t. Cajun seasoning

Optional: 1/8 t. cayenne pepper
14-1/2 oz. can fire-roasted or
    plain diced tomatoes
1-1/2 c. chicken broth
3/4 c. long-cooking rice,
    uncooked

Heat oil in a large skillet over medium-high heat. Add onion, peppers and sausage; sprinkle with desired seasonings. Sauté until onion is translucent, peppers have softened and sausage is lightly golden. Add undrained tomatoes, broth and uncooked rice. Bring to a fast simmer; turn heat to medium-low and cover. Cook for 20 minutes, or until all liquid is absorbed and rice is tender. Serves 4.

No matter what looms ahead, if you can eat today, enjoy today, mix good cheer with friends today, enjoy it and bless God for it.

– Henry Ward Beecher

Speedy Sausage Ravioli

Tracee Cummins
Amarillo, TX

This quick recipe is great for busy nights...it's light on the budget too!

1 lb. ground pork sausage	1/2 t. dried oregano
1/2 c. onion, chopped	2 15-oz. cans ravioli in sauce
1/2 t. garlic salt	1 c. shredded mozzarella cheese

Crumble sausage into a skillet; add onion. Cook over medium-high heat until sausage is no longer pink; drain. Sprinkle with seasonings; stir in ravioli. Heat through over low heat. Sprinkle with cheese; cook just until cheese melts. Makes 6 servings.

Nacho Kielbasa & Noodles

Judy Lange
Imperial, PA

Wonderful on a cold evening!

16-oz. pkg. medium egg noodles, uncooked	1 onion, chopped
1 lb. Kielbasa sausage, sliced	2 T. butter
1 green pepper, chopped	2 10-3/4 oz. cans nacho cheese or Cheddar cheese soup

Cook noodles according to package directions; drain and return to saucepan. Meanwhile, in a skillet over medium heat, cook sausage, green pepper and onion until vegetables are soft. Add sausage mixture, butter and soup to noodles. Mix thoroughly; heat until warmed through. Makes 4 servings.

Tuck packets of gravy and seasoning mix into a napkin holder
to keep the pantry tidy.

Mom's Spaghetti & Meatballs

Elaine Lucas
Runge, TX

This started out with my mom's recipe. Over the years I made it my own and it has become a family favorite...my adult children still ask me to make it when they come to visit. It's easily doubled, which is a must whenever the whole family is together!

2 8-oz. cans tomato sauce
1/2 t. garlic powder
1/2 t. dried oregano

1/2 t. dried basil
16-oz. pkg. spaghetti, uncooked

In a large skillet over medium-low heat, combine tomato sauce and seasonings. Simmer while making meatballs. Add uncooked meatballs to simmering sauce. Simmer over medium-low heat for about 30 minutes, turning meatballs over once after 15 minutes. Meanwhile, cook spaghetti according to package directions; drain. Serve sauce and meatballs over spaghetti. Serves 4.

Meatballs:

1 lb. lean ground beef
1/2 c. shredded Cheddar cheese
2 eggs, beaten

1 slice white bread, crumbled
1/2 t. garlic salt

Combine all ingredients in a large bowl; mix well. Form into one- to 2-inch balls.

For flavorful, fast-fix garlic bread, brush Italian bread slices with softened butter. Sprinkle on garlic & herb seasoning blend and broil until golden.

Rosemary Peppers & Fusilli

Jennifer Niemi
Nova Scotia, Canada

This colorful, flavorful meatless meal is ready to serve in a jiffy.

12-oz. pkg. fusilli or rotini
   pasta, uncooked
2 to 4 T. olive oil
2 red onions, thinly sliced and
   separated into rings
3 red, orange and/or yellow
   peppers, very thinly sliced

5 to 6 cloves garlic, very thinly
   sliced
3 T. dried rosemary
salt and pepper to taste
Garnish: shredded mozzarella
   cheese

Cook pasta according to package directions; drain. While pasta is cooking, coat the bottom of a large, heavy skillet well with oil. Add onions; cover and cook over medium heat for 10 minutes. Stir in remaining ingredients except cheese. Reduce heat. Cook, covered, an additional 20 minutes. Serve vegetable mixture over pasta, topped with cheese. Makes 4 servings.

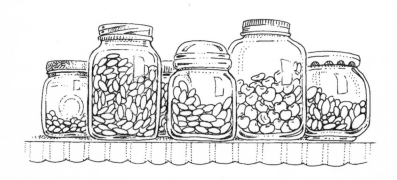

Watch for old-fashioned clear glass canisters at tag sales
and flea markets...perfect countertop storage for
pasta and dried beans.

Spanish Omelette

Elaine Day
Essex, England

This is a great big thick cake of an omelette packed with vegetables and cheese. It can be served warm as a main course, and tastes just as good cold. You can even take it on a picnic. Serve in hearty wedges with a chunky tomato & onion salad...delicious!

4 T. olive oil, divided
1 to 2 potatoes, peeled and diced
1 onion, sliced
1 red pepper, diced
1 green pepper, diced
1 zucchini, coarsely chopped

1/3 to 1/2 c. frozen peas
1/4 lb. smoked chorizo or
   Kielbasa sausage, diced
5 eggs, lightly beaten
salt and pepper to taste
1/2 c. shredded Cheddar cheese

Heat 2 tablespoons oil in an oven-proof skillet over high heat. Add potatoes and onion; toss to coat well. Reduce heat to medium-low. Cover and cook for 15 minutes, stirring occasionally. Add peppers, zucchini, peas and sausage; mix well. Cover and cook an additional 5 to 8 minutes, until vegetables start to soften. In a large bowl, combine eggs, salt and pepper. Remove skillet from heat; slowly pour vegetable mixture into bowl with eggs. Return empty skillet to stove; add remaining oil and heat over medium-high heat. Pour egg and vegetable mixture into skillet; cook for one minute. Reduce heat to low; cook, uncovered, for 15 to 20 minutes. Sprinkle omelette with cheese; place under broiler for 3 to 5 minutes, until golden and bubbly. Cut into wedges to serve. Makes 4 servings.

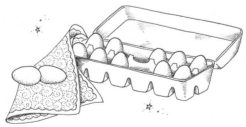

When breaking eggs, if part of a broken eggshell makes its way into the bowl, just dip in a clean eggshell half. The broken bit will grab onto it like a magnet!

Mama's Quick Meatball Subs

Cris Goode
Mooresville, IN

We love our local sub shop's French bread. We often buy day-old loaves for a delicious way to dress up this yummy family treat.

1 lb. extra-lean ground beef
1/2 sleeve saltine crackers,
   crushed
12-oz. bottle chili sauce, divided
1/4 c. reduced-fat grated
   Parmesan cheese

2 egg whites, beaten
salt and pepper to taste
15-oz. jar pizza sauce, warmed
2 loaves French bread, halved
   and split
8 slices favorite cheese

In a bowl, combine beef, cracker crumbs, half of chili sauce, Parmesan cheese, egg whites, salt and pepper. Mix well; form into sixteen, 1-1/2 inch meatballs. Place on a baking sheet sprayed with non-stick vegetable spray. Bake at 400 degrees for 15 minutes, or until golden, turning meatballs halfway through. Add baked meatballs to warmed sauce. Fill each half-loaf with 2 cheese slices and 4 meatballs. Serve with remaining chili sauce on the side. Serves 4.

Saucy sandwiches are best served on a vintage-style oilcloth...spills wipe right up! Look for one with a colorful design of fruit or flowers.

Make-Ahead Pizza Burgers

Carrie Fostor
Baltic, OH

My mom used to make these tasty sandwiches often when we were kids. They're terrific to have on hand, especially when there are hungry teenagers in the house!

1 lb. ground beef
1 onion, chopped
1/2 green pepper, chopped
2 6-inch pepperoni sticks,
   ground or finely chopped
16-oz. jar pizza sauce
1 c. shredded mozzarella cheese

4 t. dried oregano or basil
1/8 t. garlic salt
Optional: 4-oz. can sliced
   mushrooms, drained
1/4 c. butter, softened
20 hamburger buns, split

In a skillet over medium heat, brown beef, onion and green pepper; drain. Stir in remaining ingredients except butter and buns; cook for several minutes, until cheese melts. Brush butter over cut sides of buns. Divide beef mixture among the bun bottoms; add tops. Burgers may be served immediately, or wrapped individually in aluminum foil and placed in the freezer. To serve if frozen: thaw in refrigerator overnight, or let stand at room temperature about 2 hours before serving. Bake foil-wrapped burgers at 350 degrees for 15 to 20 minutes, until heated through. Makes 20 servings.

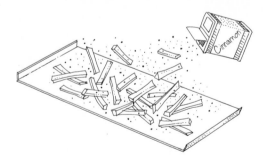

Sweet potato fries are deliciously different! Slice sweet potatoes into wedges, toss with olive oil and place on a baking sheet. Bake at 400 degrees for 20 to 30 minutes until tender, turning once. Sprinkle with a little cinnamon-sugar and serve warm.

Layered Tortilla Pie

Katy Thompson
Cartersville, GA

This recipe is very kid-friendly...my kids love it! Use purchased enchilada sauce and guacamole or your very own homemade sauces...either way, it'll be delicious.

1 lb. boneless chicken or beef, cut into strips
1 to 2 t. oil
1 c. enchilada sauce
1 t. chili powder
1/2 t. ground cumin
3/4 to 1 c. canned black beans, drained

3/4 to 1 c. canned refried beans
8 8-inch flour tortillas
1 c. guacamole, divided
8-oz. pkg. shredded Mexican-blend cheese, divided
Garnish: sour cream, salsa, guacamole

In a skillet over medium heat, brown meat in oil; drain. Stir in enchilada sauce and seasonings; remove from heat. In a separate bowl, combine beans; stir well and set aside. Place a tortilla in a lightly greased 9" round cake pan; spread with half of bean mixture. Top with another tortilla and half of meat mixture. Add another tortilla and half of guacamole. Add another tortilla and half of cheese. Top with another tortilla. Repeat layers with remaining ingredients except cheese; pan will be full. Cover with aluminum foil. Bake at 350 degrees for 30 minutes. Uncover; sprinkle with remaining cheese. Bake, uncovered, an additional 3 to 5 minutes, until cheese is melted. Cut into wedges. Serve garnished with favorite toppings. Serves 4.

Whip up a zippy Tex-Mex side dish pronto! Prepare instant rice, using chicken broth instead of water. Stir in a generous dollop of spicy salsa, top with shredded cheese and cover until cheese melts.

Chicken Enchilada Bake

Sara Wright
Colorado Springs, CO

One evening I was in the mood for Mexican food, but didn't have any taco shells or tortillas in the pantry. I decided to try using pasta...my family really enjoyed this new dish!

2 c. rotini pasta, uncooked
1 lb. boneless, skinless chicken
   breasts, cooked and chopped
15-oz. can diced tomatoes,
   drained

1-1/2 c. shredded
   Mexican-blend cheese,
   divided
10-oz. can enchilada sauce

Cook pasta according to package directions; drain. In a large bowl, combine cooked pasta, chicken, tomatoes and one cup cheese; stir in enchilada sauce. Spoon into a greased 2-quart casserole dish. Bake, uncovered, at 350 degrees for 20 to 25 minutes, until heated through and cheese is melted. Top with remaining cheese. Return to oven an additional 2 to 3 minutes, until cheese is melted. Makes 6 servings.

Serve your family dinner in an unexpected place, just for fun...a blanket in the backyard, a spread in the living room or even on the front porch. It's quick & easy with a one-dish dinner and a delightful change from routine!

Mary's Broiled Steak Tips

Beth McCarthy
Nashua, NH

A family tradition! A friend of my mother's shared this scrumptious recipe with her when my younger brother was six years old. Now he's thirty and we all still use this recipe, even though we live apart. We expect that it will be passed down to our next generation.

1 to 2 lbs. beef steak tips
1 to 2 8-oz. bottles Italian
   salad dressing
2 tomatoes, diced
1 green pepper, chopped
1 onion, chopped
Optional: 16-oz. can whole
   potatoes, drained

Optional: zucchini, yellow
   squash or other favorite
   vegetables, cut up
garlic powder, salt and pepper
   to taste
mashed potatoes or rice pilaf

In a large dish, cover steak tips with salad dressing; cover. Refrigerate overnight to marinate; drain and discard dressing. Place steak tips on a broiler pan along with tomatoes, green pepper, onion and any other desired vegetables. Season with garlic powder, salt and pepper. Broil to desired doneness, turning occasionally, about 5 to 8 minutes per side. Serve with mashed potatoes or rice pilaf. Makes 4 to 6 servings.

Cheese always makes dinner tastier! Split brown & serve dinner rolls partly in half and sprinkle shredded Cheddar or Swiss cheese and chopped green onion inside. Press halves together and bake as package directs, until golden.

Shrimp Scampi

Vickie

Spoil your family a little! This dish seems so fancy, yet is simple to make. Serve it over quick-cooking angel hair pasta for a memorable meal in minutes.

2 lbs. uncooked, peeled large
   shrimp
1/2 c. butter
1/2 c. oil
2 T. white wine or lemon juice
1/4 c. green onion, minced

1/4 c. fresh parsley, minced
1 T. garlic, minced
1 t. salt
pepper to taste
Optional: lemon wedges

Place shrimp in a large bowl; set aside. In a saucepan over medium-low heat, combine remaining ingredients except lemon wedges. Cook for 3 to 4 minutes, stirring often, until well-blended. Pour most of butter mixture over shrimp; toss to coat well. Arrange shrimp on a 15"x10" jelly-roll pan in a single layer. Broil 3 to 4 inches from heat for about 5 minutes. Transfer shrimp to a serving platter; drizzle with remaining butter mixture. Serve with lemon wedges, if desired. Serves 6.

Try a new side dish tonight...barley pilaf. Simply prepare quick-cooking barley with chicken broth instead of water, seasoning it with a little chopped onion and parsley. Filling, quick and tasty!

Deep-Dish Skillet Pizza

Linda Kilgore
Kittanning, PA

*This recipe is my husband's. He made us one of these pizzas for supper
and now it's the only pizza we ever want to eat. Delicious!*

1 loaf frozen bread dough,
 thawed
1 to 2 15-oz. jars pizza sauce
1/2 lb. ground pork sausage,
 browned and drained
5-oz. pkg. sliced pepperoni

1/2 c. sliced mushrooms
1/2 c. green pepper, sliced
Italian seasoning to taste
1 c. shredded mozzarella cheese
1 c. shredded Cheddar cheese

Generously grease a large cast-iron skillet. Press thawed dough into
the bottom and up the sides of skillet. Spread desired amount of pizza
sauce over dough. Add favorite toppings, ending with cheeses on top.
Bake at 425 degrees for 30 minutes. Carefully remove skillet from
oven. Let stand several minutes; pizza will finish baking in the skillet.
Cut into wedges to serve. Serves 4.

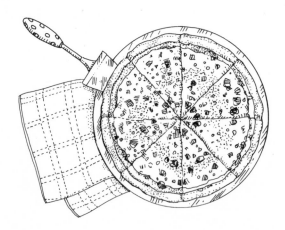

Make assembly part of pizza night fun! Prepare the crust,
then set out the sauce, pepperoni, veggies, seasonings and cheese.
Let family members add toppings as they like...even little ones
can help out. Bake, slice into quarters and dinner's ready!

One-Dish Dinners

Spaghetti Amore

Marietta Forrester
Tulsa, OK

This recipe was a favorite when our two children were growing up in the 1960s, then with the grandchildren as they came along. I still make this for Sunday dinners after church, except now I have to make a double batch for it to go around!

8-oz. pkg. spaghetti, uncooked
1 lb. ground beef
2 T. oil
1/2 c. onion, chopped
Optional: 1/4 c. green pepper,
   chopped
1 clove garlic, minced

10-3/4 oz. can cream of
   mushroom soup
10-3/4 oz. can tomato soup
1-1/4 c. water
1 c. shredded sharp Cheddar
   cheese, divided

Cook spaghetti as directed on package; drain. Meanwhile, in a skillet over medium heat, brown beef in oil with onion and green pepper, if using; drain. Stir garlic, soups and water into beef mixture. Place spaghetti in a lightly greased 13"x9" baking pan. Add beef mixture and 1/2 cup cheese; toss to mix. Bake, uncovered, at 350 degrees for 30 minutes, or until bubbly. Sprinkle remaining cheese on top. Bake for another 5 to 10 minutes, until cheese melts. Serves 4 to 6.

To test for doneness, insert the tip of a table knife in the center of a casserole. If the knife tip is hot to the touch when pulled out, the casserole should be heated through. Good to know when baking a casserole that's been made ahead and stored in the fridge.

Mama's Mucho Nachos

Janie Branstetter
Duncan, OK

This may sound like an appetizer, but it's really a meal in itself!
Add a crisp green salad and some fresh fruit for a dinner
the whole family will love.

6-oz. pkg. tortilla chips
3 c. shredded Cheddar-Jack
   cheese, divided
15-1/2 oz. can fat-free refried
   beans
1 c. chunky salsa or picante
   sauce

1 lb. ground pork sausage,
   browned and drained
1 bunch green onions, chopped
1 to 2 tomatoes, chopped
Garnish: sour cream, sliced
   jalapeño peppers

In a greased deep 13"x9" baking pan, place a layer of tortilla chips.
Top with 1-1/2 cups cheese, refried beans and salsa or sauce. Sprinkle
with sausage and remaining cheese. Bake, uncovered, at 350 degrees
for 10 to 20 minutes, until heated through and cheese is melted.
Remove from oven. Top with onions and tomatoes; add sour cream
and jalapeño peppers, as desired. Serves 4 to 6.

Bored with tacos? Serve Mexican-style sandwiches for a tasty
change! Called tortas, they're hollowed-out crusty bread rolls
stuffed with shredded beef or pork and cheese. Serve cold or
toast like a panini sandwich...yum!

Taco Hot Dish

Julie Snow
Park Rapids, MN

When I was growing up, we got this recipe from one of my brother's friends. It was an instant favorite...we still remember him because of it! Now my kids request it all the time. Guests love it too. I hope you enjoy it as much as we do!

1 lb. ground beef
1-1/4 oz. pkg. taco seasoning
  mix
1/2 c. water
15-1/2 oz. can refried beans
8-oz. tube refrigerated crescent
  rolls

6-oz. pkg. corn chips, crushed
  and divided
16-oz. container sour cream
2 c. shredded Cheddar cheese
Optional: salsa, shredded
  lettuce, chopped tomatoes

Brown beef in a skillet over medium heat; drain. Add taco seasoning, water and beans to skillet; simmer 5 minutes. Press crescent rolls into the bottom of an ungreased 13"x9" baking pan; add half of crushed corn chips. Spread beef mixture over chips; top with sour cream, cheese and remaining corn chips. Bake, uncovered, at 350 degrees for 30 minutes. Let stand 10 minutes. Cut into squares to serve; garnish as desired. Serves 6.

Make your own taco seasoning mix...it's easily adjusted to your family's taste. In a large jar, combine 3/4 cup dried, minced onion; 1/4 cup each salt and chili powder, 2 tablespoons each cornstarch, red pepper flakes, ground cumin and dried, minced garlic; and one tablespoon dried oregano. Four tablespoons of mix equals a 1-1/4 ounce envelope.

Swiss Ham Buns

Rebecca Geyer
Bremen, IN

My late grandmother gave this recipe to me. It's one I like to make and take to the fields during spring planting. The buns can be made ahead and wrapped, then baked at serving time.

1/4 c. mustard
1/4 c. mayonnaise-type salad
    dressing
2 T. onion, finely chopped
1/2 t. salt

1/8 t. pepper
12 hamburger buns, split
12 slices deli ham
12 slices baby Swiss cheese

Mix together mustard, salad dressing, onion, salt and pepper. Spread mixture on cut sides of buns. Top each bun with one slice of ham and one slice of cheese. Wrap buns individually in aluminum foil; place on a baking sheet. Bake at 350 degrees for 25 minutes. Serve hot. Makes 12 servings.

It's easy to shake up sandwiches at dinnertime...just offer a variety of breads to choose from. Focaccia, rye, pumpernickel, pita rounds and whole-wheat bread all make terrifically tasty sandwiches!

Reuben Casserole

Debbie Dowen
Schodack Landing, NY

A hearty, quick go-to casserole that's a family favorite!

3/4 lb. sliced deli corned beef,
   cut into 1/2-inch squares
28-oz. can sauerkraut, drained
   and squeezed dry
1 tomato, diced

1/2 c. mayonnaise
1/4 c. catsup
4 slices Swiss cheese
6 slices rye bread, toasted

In a bowl, combine corned beef, sauerkraut and tomato. In a separate small bowl, mix together mayonnaise and catsup; add to corned beef mixture and mix well. Spread in a lightly greased 8"x8" baking pan; top with cheese slices. Bake, uncovered, at 425 degrees for 15 to 20 minutes, or until cheese is bubbly. Let cool for a few minutes. Serve hot corned beef mixture open-faced on slices of toast, with Oven Fries on the side. Makes 6 servings.

Oven Fries:

2 to 3 russet potatoes, peeled
   and cut into 1/2-inch cubes

1 T. oil
salt or seasoning salt to taste

In a bowl; toss potato cubes in oil; add salt to taste. Spread on a baking sheet. Bake at 425 degrees for 20 to 30 minutes, until tender and golden.

Some like it hot! There are lots of ways to turn up the heat
in familiar recipes...hot pepper sauce, spicy salsa, creamy
horseradish, hot Chinese mustard or Japanese wasabi.
Try 'em all...see what you like best!

Tuna Tetrazzini

Nancy Gasko
South Bend, IN

*Stir in a small box of frozen peas to make this hearty
casserole a complete meal.*

8-oz. pkg. spaghetti, uncooked
4-oz. can sliced mushrooms,
    drained
1/4 c. butter
2 10-3/4 oz. cans cream of
    mushroom soup
3/4 c. milk

1/4 c. sherry or water
1/2 t. garlic salt
1/4 to 1/2 t. onion powder
1 c. shredded Cheddar cheese
2 6-oz. cans tuna, drained
Garnish: dry bread crumbs,
    grated Parmesan cheese

Cook spaghetti as directed on package; drain. Meanwhile, in a Dutch
oven over medium heat, sauté mushrooms in butter. Stir in remaining
ingredients except tuna and garnish. Add cooked spaghetti and tuna;
toss to mix well. Transfer to a 3-quart casserole dish coated with
non-stick vegetable spray. Top with bread crumbs and Parmesan
cheese. Bake, uncovered, at 400 degrees for 30 minutes, until heated
through and golden. Serves 4 to 6.

It's simple to make your own bread crumbs for crunchy casserole
toppings. Save extra bread slices (leftover "heels" are fine) and
freeze in a plastic bag. When you have enough, bake the slices
in a 250-degree oven until dry and crumbly, then tear into
sections and pulse in a food processor or blender.

Spiced-Up Tuna Noodle Casserole
Elizabeth Kolberg
Tolland, CT

Mom always made tuna noodle casserole and this is her recipe...but updated for some of us kids who liked things a bit spicier! I made this dish quite a bit during college and everyone always wanted more.

8-oz. pkg. medium egg noodles,
  uncooked
2 6-oz. cans tuna, drained
10-3/4 oz. can cream of
  mushroom soup
1-1/2 c. shredded Pepper Jack
  cheese

4-oz. can sliced mushrooms,
  drained
3 green onions, sliced
hot pepper sauce to taste
1-1/2 c. potato chips, crushed
  and divided

Cook noodles according to package directions; drain. Meanwhile, in a bowl, mix together remaining ingredients, reserving 1/2 cup crushed potato chips for topping. Mix in cooked noodles. Spread mixture into a greased 9"x9" baking pan; top with reserved potato chips. Bake, uncovered, at 350 degrees for 30 to 40 minutes, until hot and bubbly. Serves 4.

A busy-day hint...if family members will be eating at different times, spoon casserole ingredients into individual ramekins for baking. Each person can enjoy their own fresh-from-the-oven mini casserole.

Hearty Wild Rice Dinner

Kay Marone
Des Moines, IA

Our favorite after-Thanksgiving recipe...the rest of the time, we make it with chicken. It's too yummy to enjoy only once a year!

6-1/2 oz. pkg. quick-cooking
   long-grain and wild rice
3/4 lb. ground pork sausage
1 c. onion, chopped
8-oz. can sliced mushrooms,
   drained
8-oz. can sliced water chestnuts,
   drained

1/4 c. all-purpose flour
1/8 t. pepper
1-1/2 c. chicken broth
3/4 c. milk
2 c. cooked turkey or chicken,
   cubed

Cook rice according to package directions. Meanwhile, in a skillet over medium heat, brown sausage and onion; drain. Add mushrooms, water chestnuts, flour and pepper; mix well. Add broth and milk; cook and stir until mixture is thickened and bubbly. Continue cooking and stirring for one minute. Toss together sausage mixture, cooked rice and turkey or chicken. Place in a greased 3-quart casserole dish. Bake, uncovered, at 350 degrees for 25 to 30 minutes, until hot and bubbly. Serves 6.

While the casserole bakes, steam fresh broccoli, green beans or zucchini in the microwave. Place cut-up veggies in a microwave-safe container and add a little water. Cover with plastic wrap, venting with a knife tip. Microwave on high for 2 to 5 minutes, checking for tenderness after each minute. Uncover carefully to allow hot steam to escape.

One-Dish Dinners

Crumbed Honey Mustard Pork Chops

Sarina Skidmore
Urbana, MO

Just three ingredients...what could be easier?

8-oz. pkg. cornbread stuffing
  mix

1/2 c. honey mustard
4 to 6 pork chops

Pour stuffing mix into a shallow dish; set aside. Brush mustard over both sides of each pork chop; coat with stuffing mix. Arrange pork chops on a lightly greased baking sheet. Bake, uncovered, at 350 degrees for 20 minutes, or until juices run clear. Serves 4 to 6.

Hearty Pork Chops & Rice

Wanda Rhoades
San Antonio, TX

This recipe came from an Air Force friend in the 1970s. For a different dish, use boneless chicken and chicken broth.

2 c. instant rice, uncooked
8 pork chops
1 to 2 T. oil

2 10-1/2 oz. cans beef broth
2-1/2 c. water

Add rice to a lightly greased 13"x9" baking pan; set aside. In a large skillet over medium heat, brown pork chops on both sides in oil; drain. Arrange pork chops on top of rice. In a bowl, whisk broth and water together; spoon over pork chops. Cover tightly with aluminum foil. Bake at 425 degrees for 35 minutes, or until pork chop juices run clear and rice is tender. Serves 6 to 8.

No peeking when there's a casserole in the oven! Every time the oven door is opened, the temperature drops at least 25 degrees... dinner will take longer to bake.

Beefy Hashbrown Bake

Sue Klapper
Muskego, WI

A tasty meal-in-a-pan that my family and I really enjoy.

4 c. frozen shredded
   hashbrowns
3 T. oil
1/8 t. pepper
1 lb. ground beef
1 c. water
.87-oz. pkg. brown gravy mix

1/2 t. garlic salt
2 c. frozen mixed vegetables
2.8-oz. can French fried onions,
   divided
1 c. shredded Cheddar cheese,
   divided

In a bowl, combine frozen hashbrowns, oil and pepper. Press into a greased 8"x8" baking pan. Bake, uncovered, at 350 degrees for 15 to 20 minutes, or until hashbrowns are thawed and set. Meanwhile, in a skillet over medium heat, brown beef; drain. Add water, gravy mix and garlic salt to skillet. Bring to a boil; cook and stir for 2 minutes. Add frozen vegetables; cook and stir for 5 minutes. Stir in half of the onions and 1/2 cup cheese. Pour beef mixture over hashbrowns. Bake, uncovered, at 350 degrees for 5 to 10 minutes. Sprinkle with remaining onions and cheese; bake 5 minutes longer, or until cheese melts. Makes 4 servings.

Create a game of table talk! Make up some fun questions to write on file cards...What's your favorite book? Where would you like to travel to? and so on. Pull a different card each night to discuss at dinnertime.

One-Dish Dinners

Tasty Cheesy Bake

Janie Reed
Zanesville, OH

This simple recipe is easy to modify with what you have on hand. I've used both sausage and shredded chicken instead of ground beef, and a Colby blend works fine in place of the Cheddar. The dish comes out all cheesy goodness with crispy, crusty edges. Yum!

1/2 c. margarine
5 slices bread, toasted
1 lb. ground beef, browned and
    drained
1/2 c. onion, chopped

1 T. prepared mustard
1/2 c. milk
3 eggs, lightly beaten
1 T. dry mustard
2 c. shredded Cheddar cheese

Spread margarine on both sides of toast slices; set aside. Combine beef, onion and prepared mustard. In a separate bowl, whisk together milk, eggs and dry mustard; set aside. In a lightly greased 8"x8" baking pan, layer half of toast, half of beef mixture and half of cheese. Repeat layers; pour milk mixture over top. Bake, uncovered, at 350 degrees for 30 minutes, or until top is golden and cheese is bubbly.
Serves 4 to 6.

Clean baked-on food from a casserole dish...no elbow grease required! Place a dryer sheet in the dish and fill with warm water. Let the dish sit overnight, then sponge clean. You'll find the fabric softeners will really soften the baked-on food!

Good Ol' Beans & Hot Dogs

Marilyn Morel
Keene, NH

*A great-tasting dish to make after a busy day. My guys love hot dogs
and baked beans, so this is always a big hit. Add a favorite veggie and
cinnamon applesauce for a tasty meal!*

2 T. butter
1 onion, chopped
1 green pepper, chopped
1 lb. hot dogs, thinly sliced
2 28-oz. cans baked beans

1/4 c. catsup
1/4 c. light brown sugar, packed
2 t. deli-style mustard
4 slices bacon

Melt butter in a skillet over medium heat; sauté onion and green
pepper until tender. Add hot dogs. Sauté until hot dogs are lightly
golden; remove from heat. In a lightly greased 3-quart casserole dish,
combine hot dog mixture and remaining ingredients except bacon.
Stir until well blended. Lay bacon slices over top of casserole. Bake,
uncovered, at 350 degrees for 30 to 45 minutes, until hot and bubbly.
Makes 4 to 6 servings.

Set a regular theme for each night of the week...Italian Night,
Soup & Salad Night, Mexican Night or Casserole Night, based on
your family's favorites. Meal planning will be a snap!

Slow Cookers
to the
Rescue

Beef Tips & Noodles

Suzette Rummell
Cuyahoga Falls, OH

This is my daughter's favorite dinner when she comes home from college. She always lets me know to put it on the menu before she arrives. We like to use Amish-made egg noodles.

3 to 4-lb. beef chuck roast, cubed
salt and pepper to taste
10-3/4 oz. can golden mushroom soup
10-3/4 oz. can cream of mushroom soup
2-1/2 c. water

.53-oz. pkg. French onion soup mix or 1 onion, chopped
2 T. all-purpose flour
3 T. cold water
8-oz. container sour cream
8-oz. pkg. medium egg noodles, cooked

Season beef cubes with salt and pepper; place in a slow cooker. In a separate bowl, stir together soups, water and soup mix or onion; add to slow cooker. Cover and cook on high setting for 6 to 7 hours, until beef is tender. In a small bowl, stir flour into water; add to slow cooker and stir gently. Cover and cook on high setting to desired gravy consistency, about 15 minutes. Just before serving, stir in sour cream. Serve beef and gravy over cooked noodles. Serves 6.

With work, school and after-school activities, dinner can be a challenge. Now's the time to get out that slow cooker! Other than a quick chop of a few ingredients, recipes are usually a simple matter of tossing everything into the pot.

Slow Cookers
to the *Rescue*

Italian Beef Au Jus

Tami Arsenault
Nashua, NH

This delicious roast is requested often. It's easy to make...the slow cooker does all the work! I serve it as a main dish with potatoes and a green vegetable...very satisfying.

3 to 4-lb. beef rump roast, trimmed
14-oz. can beef broth
1/2 c. plus 2 T. water

1-oz. pkg. au jus gravy mix
1-oz. pkg. Italian salad dressing mix

Place roast in a slow cooker. Combine remaining ingredients and pour over beef. Cover and cook on low setting for 8 hours, or until beef is very tender. Makes 6 to 8 servings.

Slow-cooked beef chuck roast is always a winner! Any leftovers will be equally delicious in sandwiches, soups or casseroles, so be sure to choose the largest size roast your slow cooker will hold.

Easy Cheesy Enchiladas

Julie Green
Blackwell, OK

*After trying several slow-cooker enchilada recipes, I started
experimenting and this was the tasty result. My husband loves it.
I like to use different cheeses on each layer...yum!*

1 lb. ground beef
10-3/4 oz. can cream of chicken
  soup
10-oz. can enchilada sauce
1.35-oz. pkg. onion soup mix

5 to 6 6-inch fajita-size flour
  tortillas
1/4 lb. pasteurized process
  cheese spread, cubed
1 c. shredded Cheddar cheese

Brown beef in a skillet over medium heat; drain. Stir in soup, sauce
and soup mix. In a slow cooker, layer some of the beef mixture, one
tortilla and some of the cubed cheese. Repeat layers with remaining
beef mixture, tortillas and cubed cheese. Top with shredded cheese.
Cover and cook on low setting for 2 to 3 hours, until hot and bubbly.
Serves 4 to 6.

If you only use part of a package of tortillas, it's fine to freeze
the leftover ones in an airtight container. For the best texture,
let them thaw overnight in the fridge before using.

Tortellini Broccoli Alfredo

Theresa Wehmeyer
Rosebud, MO

This easy meal really satisfies our family. It's perfect for Lent or other times we just want to enjoy a meatless meal. You don't even need to thaw the tortellini or the broccoli.

2 16-oz. jars Alfredo sauce
1/2 c. water
20-oz. pkg. frozen cheese-filled
   tortellini

16-oz. pkg. frozen broccoli
   flowerets

In a bowl, stir together sauce and water. Layer ingredients in a slow cooker as follows: 1/3 of the sauce, all of the frozen tortellini, 1/3 of the sauce and all of the frozen broccoli. Pour remaining sauce over the broccoli. Cover and cook on high setting for 3 hours, until heated through. Makes 8 servings.

Pick up a bundle of fresh flowers when you shop for groceries.
Tucked into a pitcher or glass jar, even simple daisies
are charming and cheerful!

Lemonade Chicken

Kathy Werner
Minneola, FL

Everyone loves this chicken! My girls are now on their own,
and this is one of the first recipes I gave them.

6 skinless chicken thighs
1/2 c. all-purpose flour
1 t. salt
1 to 2 T. oil
6-oz. can frozen lemonade
   concentrate

3 T. brown sugar, packed
3 T. catsup
1 t. balsamic vinegar or cider
   vinegar
2 T. cornstarch
1/4 c. cold water

Dredge chicken in flour mixed with salt. In a skillet over medium heat, cook chicken in oil until golden; drain. Transfer chicken to a slow cooker. Mix lemonade, brown sugar, catsup and vinegar; pour over chicken. Cover and cook on low setting for 6 to 8 hours, or on high setting for 3 to 4 hours. Remove chicken to a platter; keep warm. Whisk cornstarch into cold water; add to juices in slow cooker. Cover and cook on high setting to desired sauce consistency, about 15 minutes. Serve chicken with sauce. Makes 6 servings.

Chicken Yum-Yum

Sandra Bonander
Modesto, CA

When you feed this to your kids, their friends will want to stay for
dinner...because you have the house with the best food!

4 to 6 boneless, skinless
   chicken breasts
salt and pepper to taste
8-oz. container sour cream

10-3/4 oz. can cream of chicken
   soup
1.35-oz. pkg. onion soup mix
cooked egg noodles or rice

Arrange chicken in a slow cooker; sprinkle with salt and pepper. Mix sour cream, soup and soup mix together; spread over chicken. Cover and cook on low setting for 4 to 6 hours. Serve chicken over cooked noodles or rice, topped with some of the sauce. Serves 4 to 6.

Herb Garden Chicken

Julie Neff
Citrus Springs, FL

This is the chicken dish my husband asks for most often.

4 to 6 boneless, skinless
   chicken breasts
2 tomatoes, chopped
1 onion, chopped
2 cloves garlic, chopped
2/3 c. chicken broth
1 bay leaf

1 t. dried thyme
1-1/2 t. salt
1 t. pepper, or more to taste
2 c. broccoli flowerets
Optional: 2 to 3 T. all-purpose
   flour
cooked rice

Place chicken in a slow cooker; top with tomatoes, onion and garlic. Combine broth and seasonings; pour over chicken. Cover and cook on low setting for 8 hours. Add broccoli; cook for one additional hour, or until chicken juices run clear and broccoli is tender. Juices in slow cooker may be thickened with a little flour, if desired. Discard bay leaf; serve over cooked rice. Makes 4 to 6 servings.

"Hot Wing" Spicy Chicken

Kathy Skogen
Peoria, AZ

We love hot chicken wings. This is an easy way to enjoy the same spicy flavor without the mess of the wings!

4 to 6 boneless, skinless
   chicken breasts

1 c. butter, melted
1 c. cayenne hot pepper sauce

Arrange chicken in a slow cooker. Mix melted butter and hot sauce; drizzle over chicken. Cover and cook on low setting for 5 to 6 hours. Chicken may also be baked, covered, at 350 degrees for about one hour. Serves 4 to 6.

Use acrylic paint to write "Tonight's Specials" across the top of a small slate. Use chalk to update daily...let everyone know what's for dinner!

Hawaiian Honey Pork Roast

JoAnn

Perfect for a festive meal at the end of a busy day! I like to serve buttery mashed sweet potatoes with this yummy roast.

3-lb. boneless pork roast,
   rolled and tied
5 whole cloves
1/2 t. nutmeg
1/4 t. paprika
1/4 c. catsup
2 T. orange juice

2 T. honey
1 T. soy sauce
2 t. lemon juice
1/2 t. browning and seasoning
   sauce
1-1/2 T. cornstarch
2 T. cold water

Place roast on a rack in a broiler pan. Broil for 15 to 20 minutes, or until browned. Press cloves into top of roast; sprinkle with spices. Place roast in a slow cooker. In a small bowl, stir together remaining ingredients except cornstarch and water; pour over roast. Cover and cook on low setting for 10 to 12 hours, or on high setting for 6 to 7 hours. Remove roast to a serving platter; keep warm. In a small bowl, blend cornstarch into cold water; stir into juices in slow cooker. Cover and cook on high setting to desired gravy consistency, about 15 minutes. Slice roast and serve with gravy from slow cooker. Makes 6 to 8 servings.

Add some extra pizazz to a barbecue sandwich...top it
with a scoop of creamy coleslaw.

Teriyaki Steak & Rice

Ernestine Trent
Elkview, WV

*This recipe is one of my all-time favorites. It's easy to fix and
tastes scrumptious...what more could you want?*

2 lbs. boneless beef chuck,
   sliced into thin strips
1/2 c. soy sauce
2 T. oil

1 T. sugar
1 t. ground ginger
1 clove garlic, pressed
cooked rice

Place beef strips in a slow cooker; set aside. In a small bowl, combine
remaining ingredients except rice; pour over beef and toss to coat.
Cover and cook on low setting for 6 to 8 hours. Serve beef over
cooked rice. Makes 6 servings.

Veggie sides don't need to be fancy...they don't even need to be
cooked! Make a relish tray with crunchy baby carrots, cherry
tomatoes, broccoli flowerets and a hollowed-out green pepper
filled with ranch dressing for dipping...ready to serve in a jiffy!

Sweet-and-Sour Meatballs

Lori Dobson
Ontario, Canada

My mother and I make these meatballs every year for our Christmas family reunion. They're always a hit! Don't wait for a special occasion, though...they're terrific as an everyday main dish too.

1 lb. ground beef
3/4 c. dry bread crumbs
1 egg, beaten
2 T. Worcestershire sauce
2 T. dried, minced onion
1 t. dried oregano
1/2 t. salt

1/2 t. pepper
14-oz. can pineapple tidbits,
   drained and juice reserved
1/3 c. cider vinegar
1/2 c. dark brown sugar, packed
1 T. soy sauce
1 T. cornstarch

In a bowl, combine beef, bread crumbs, egg, Worcestershire sauce, onion and seasonings. Mix well; form into walnut-size meatballs. Cook meatballs in a large skillet over medium-high heat until well browned; drain. Meanwhile, in a slow cooker on high setting, mix together reserved pineapple juice, vinegar, brown sugar and soy sauce. Stir constantly until mixture comes to a boil; add cornstarch. Stir until dissolved; continue cooking for 3 to 4 minutes. Add meatballs and pineapple; stir to coat with sauce. Cover and cook on high setting for 3 hours. Serves 6.

Post a dinner wishlist on the fridge and invite everyone to jot down their favorite dishes. Family members who are involved in meal planning are much more likely to look forward to family dinnertimes together.

Meatballs in Cream Sauce

Kathie High
Lititz, PA

One morning I looked around my kitchen, hoping a dinner idea would jump out at me. I found these ingredients and tossed them into the slow cooker. At dinner I watched my family for reactions and was pleasantly surprised to see smiles. I hope this recipe helps another busy family find smiles at dinnertime!

24 to 36 refrigerated meatballs
10-3/4 oz. can cream of
   mushroom soup
10-3/4 oz. can cream of chicken
   soup

8-oz. container sour cream
cooked egg noodles or mashed
   potatoes

Place meatballs in a slow cooker; set aside. In a bowl, stir together soups and sour cream; pour over meatballs. Cover and cook on low setting for 6 to 8 hours, or on high setting for 3 hours. Serve meatballs and sauce over cooked noodles or mashed potatoes. Serves 4 to 6.

Always keep the pantry stocked with canned vegetables, creamy soups, rice mixes, pasta and other handy meal-makers. If you pick up two or three items whenever they're on sale, you'll have a full pantry in no time at all!

Stewed Chicken Verde

Robin Acasio
Chula Vista, CA

This chicken is so tender and juicy...the leftovers make yummy quesadillas too. I love to use my slow cooker and I'm always thinking up new ideas to try. This recipe was a hit with my family a couple years ago, and I've been making it ever since!

3 to 3-1/2 lb. whole chicken
1 T. poultry seasoning
1/4 onion, sliced
several sprigs fresh cilantro

10-3/4 oz. can cream of chicken
    soup
4-oz. can chopped green chiles
cooked rice

Sprinkle chicken all over with poultry seasoning. Place onion slices and cilantro inside chicken. Place chicken in an oval slow cooker; top with soup and chiles. Cover and cook on low setting for 7 to 8 hours. Serve with cooked rice. Serves 4 to 6.

Slow cookers come in so many sizes, you might want to have more than one! A 4-quart size is handy for recipes that will feed about four people, while a 5-1/2 to 6-quart one is terrific for larger families and potluck-size recipes. Just have room for one? Choose an oval slow cooker...roasts and whole chickens will fit perfectly.

Beth's Salsa Chicken

Beth Pirnick
Clearfield, PA

This is one of my favorite slow cooker recipes. It's super simple, super quick and super delicious! Garnish it my way, or add your own toppings.

2 16-oz. jars salsa, divided
4 boneless, skinless chicken
  breasts

Garnish: corn, black beans,
  tortilla chips, sour cream,
  shredded Cheddar cheese

Pour one jar of salsa into a slow cooker. Arrange chicken breasts over salsa; cover with second jar of salsa. Cover and cook on low setting for 6 to 8 hours. Serve chicken garnished with desired toppings. Serves 4.

For a speedy side with Tex-Mex flair, dress up a 16-ounce can of refried beans...it's easy! Sauté 2 seeded and diced pickled jalapeños, 2 chopped cloves garlic and 1/4 cup chopped onion in 2 tablespoons bacon drippings. Add beans, heat through and stir in 1/2 teaspoon ground cumin.

Easy Sauerbraten Beef

*Denise Frederick
Climax, NY*

*This recipe is simply wonderful. There's a delicious aroma
when you walk into the house...and what a nice comforting meal
to have after a long day at work.*

16 gingersnap cookies
2 lbs. London broil beef steak,
   sliced into 1/2-inch thick
   strips
10-3/4 oz. can French onion
   soup

2/3 c. water
1/2 c. white vinegar
1/4 c. oil
potato pancakes or cooked
   egg noodles

Place cookies into a gallon-size plastic zipping bag and crush them.
Add beef strips to bag; close bag and shake thoroughly until coated.
Transfer the entire contents of bag into a slow cooker. In a bowl,
combine soup, water, vinegar and oil; pour over beef mixture. Cover
and cook on low setting for 6 to 8 hours. Serve over potato pancakes
or cooked noodles. Makes 4 to 6 servings.

Crispy potato pancakes are a tasty way to use up leftover
mashed potatoes...delicious alongside meals morning,
noon or night! Stir an egg yolk and some minced onion into
2 cups mashed potatoes. Form into patties and fry in
a little butter until golden on both sides.

Saucy Short Ribs

Lori Rosenberg
University Heights, OH

*These short ribs taste even better the next day! I like to cook them
a day ahead and refrigerate overnight, then any excess fat
can easily be skimmed off before reheating them.*

3 to 4 lbs. beef short ribs
1 T. butter
1 yellow onion, finely chopped
3/4 c. catsup

1/4 c. soy sauce
3 T. cider vinegar
3 T. brown sugar, packed

Place ribs on a broiler pan; broil until well browned. Meanwhile, in a
saucepan over medium heat, melt butter. Cook onion, stirring, until
soft and golden, about 5 minutes. Add remaining ingredients. Stir
until smooth; cook for 5 minutes. Arrange ribs in a slow cooker,
stacking if necessary. Spoon sauce evenly over ribs. Cover and cook
on low setting for 7 to 8 hours, until beef is tender and begins to
separate from the bone. Transfer ribs to a serving platter; keep warm.
Continue cooking sauce in slow cooker for a few minutes longer.
Spoon any fat off the surface and discard. Pour sauce over ribs to
serve. Serves 4.

Cook egg noodles the easy way, no watching needed. Bring water
to a rolling boil, then turn off heat. Add noodles and let stand
for 20 minutes, stirring twice. Drain well and toss with
a little butter...ready to serve!

Easy-Peasy Pork Chops

Carmen Hyde
Spencerville, IN

My children love these pork chops...as a matter of fact, the whole family does! A dear friend gave me the original recipe and I tweaked it to my liking. I serve them with mashed potatoes or rice topped with the gravy, a veggie side dish and hot rolls. Mmm-mmm good!

2 to 3 lbs. boneless pork chops,
   1/2-inch thick
2 10-3/4 oz. cans cream of
   chicken soup
1-2/3 c. water
6 T. Worcestershire sauce

1/4 to 1/2 t. salt
1/4 to 1/2 t. pepper
Optional: 1 T. all-purpose flour,
   1/2 c. cold water
mashed potatoes or cooked rice

Place pork chops in a slow cooker. In a bowl, mix soup, water, Worcestershire sauce, salt and pepper; pour over chops. If mixture doesn't completely cover the chops, add a little more water. Cover and cook on high setting for 4 to 6 hours. Remove chops to a serving dish; keep warm. Strain juices from slow cooker to serve as gravy. If a thicker gravy is desired, strain juices into a saucepan; combine flour and cold water in a small bowl. Add to saucepan a little at a time; cook and stir over medium heat to desired thickness. Serve pork chops with gravy and mashed potatoes or cooked rice. Makes 8 to 10 servings.

Slow-cooked meals mean less time in the kitchen...more time for family fun! Why not have the kids turn their favorite drawings into whimsical placemats? Arrange on a backing of construction paper and cover with a layer of self-adhesive clear plastic.

Lisa's Pork Barbecue

Lisa McLaughlin
Lost Creek, WV

This pork barbecue is delicious served on buns, but for a change, here's another yummy way I've discovered. Unroll a package of refrigerated crescent rolls and spoon a little BBQ onto each roll, then roll up. Bake crescents according to the package directions.

3 to 4-lb. pork loin or Boston
   butt roast
1 to 2 T. oil
1 c. vinegar
2 T. sugar
1 T. salt

1/4 to 1/2 c. catsup
1 T. Worcestershire sauce
hot pepper sauce to taste
6 to 8 hamburger buns, split
   and lightly toasted

In a skillet over medium-high heat, brown roast in oil on all sides; drain. Place roast in a slow cooker. Mix vinegar, sugar and salt in a small bowl; pour over roast. Cover and cook on low setting for 8 to 10 hours, until very tender. Remove roast from slow cooker; reserve 1/2 cup of juices from slow cooker. Discard any bones and fat; cut pork into small pieces. In a small bowl, mix reserved juice, catsup and sauces to taste. Toss mixture with pork before serving on buns. Makes 6 to 8 servings.

Start a tradition of having a regular night for dinner guests. Many slow-cooker recipes make plenty of food for sharing. Invite a neighbor or co-worker you've wanted to get to know better... encourage your kids to invite a friend. You'll be so glad you did!

Sweet Pork Barbacoa

Jill Ball
Highland, UT

Life is busy, so thank heaven for slow cookers! This is a yummy and easy recipe. I make a huge batch, then divide it and freeze for later use. The pork is terrific in burritos, toasted rolls and salads.

3-lb. boneless pork tenderloin
3 c. mild, medium or hot salsa
3/4 c. cola

1 c. brown sugar, packed
salt and pepper to taste

Place tenderloin in a slow cooker. Mix remaining ingredients and pour over tenderloin. Cover and cook on low setting for 8 hours, or until very tender. Remove pork and shred with 2 forks. Return pork to slow cooker; stir to mix with juices. Serve as desired. Serves 10 to 12.

Halftime Pork Sandwiches

JoAnna Nicoline-Haughey
Berwyn, PA

Come and get it...the sandwiches are always ready to go at halftime!

3 to 4-lb. boneless center-cut
  pork loin
4 to 5 cloves garlic
2 to 3 T. olive oil
salt and pepper to taste

6 to 8 kaiser rolls, split
7-oz. jar roasted red peppers,
  drained
1/2 lb. sliced provolone cheese

Make 4 to 5 tiny slits in pork loin with a knife tip; insert garlic cloves. Place pork loin in a slow cooker. Drizzle with olive oil; sprinkle with salt and pepper. Cover and cook on low setting for 8 to 9 hours. Shred pork with 2 forks. Serve on kaiser rolls, topped with red peppers and cheese. Makes 6 to 8 servings.

Rolls and buns filled with juicy, slow-cooked meat
will drip less if they're toasted first.

So-Good Barbecue Buns

Kelly Bartels
Mount Orab, OH

You might as well double this recipe...everyone will want seconds!

1 lb. ground beef, browned
   and drained
1 onion, chopped
1 green pepper, chopped
2 stalks celery, chopped
Optional: 1 T. jalapeño peppers,
   chopped

12-oz. bottle chili sauce
1-1/2 t. mustard
1 t. vinegar
1 t. salt
1/2 t. ground cloves
4 hamburger buns, split

Combine all ingredients except buns in a slow cooker; mix well.
Cover and cook on low setting for 4 hours. Serve on buns.
Makes 4 servings.

A terrific way to "beef up" any recipe...crumble leftover meatloaf
or cut roast beef into bite-size pieces, season to taste and
toss into casseroles, soups and sauces.

Simple Cheeseburger Sandwiches
Patty Fosnight
Wildorado, TX

This is an awesome dinner to make on busy days, especially game days. Everyone loves these sandwiches!

1-1/2 lbs. lean ground beef
3 cloves garlic, pressed and
   divided
1/4 t. salt
1/2 t. pepper
8-oz. pkg. pasteurized process
   cheese spread, cubed

2 T. milk
1 onion, chopped
8 hamburger buns, split
Garnish: mustard, catsup,
   mayonnaise, sliced pickles,
   tomatoes and onion

In a skillet over medium heat, brown beef with one clove garlic, salt and pepper, adding a little water if needed. Drain; add beef mixture to a slow cooker. Add remaining garlic, cheese, milk and onion. Cover and cook on low setting for 6 to 7 hours. Spoon onto buns; serve with desired toppings. Makes 8 servings.

Pick up a stack of vintage plastic burger baskets. Lined with red-checked paper napkins, they're still such fun for serving hot dogs, burgers and fries...clean-up after dinner is a snap too. Don't forget the pickle!

Cordie's Famous Sloppy Joes

Pat Beach
Fisherville, KY

My mother devised this recipe when I was a child, over fifty years ago. Sometimes she served it over spaghetti instead of buns and called it Italian Spaghetti. We have served it at family get-togethers for many, many years. I hope you enjoy it as much as we have!

5 lbs. ground beef
1 to 2 onions, chopped
1 to 2 green peppers, chopped
29-oz. can tomato sauce
15-oz. can tomato sauce
1-1/4 c. catsup

1-1/4 c. brown sugar, or to
   taste, packed
1/3 c. mustard
20 to 24 hamburger buns, split
Optional: American cheese slices

In a very large skillet over medium heat, brown beef, onion and green pepper; drain. Add beef mixture to a large slow cooker. Add tomato sauce, catsup, brown sugar and mustard; stir to mix. Cover and cook on high setting for 2 hours, or until heated through, stirring after one hour. Serve on hamburger buns, garnished with a slice of cheese if desired. Makes 20 to 24 servings.

Scrumptious food tucked in your freezer is like money in the bank! Use square plastic freezer containers...they take up less room than round ones. To squeeze in even more, ladle prepared food into plastic zipping bags, seal and press flat. When frozen, they'll stack easily.

Best-Ever Shredded Beef Tacos

Kathy Lowe
Orem, UT

Two for one! The first night, I make tacos with this recipe. The second night, I add barbecue sauce to the remaining beef and make barbecue beef sandwiches. This recipe is delicious made with boneless pork or chicken too.

3 to 5-lb. beef chuck roast
1 c. water
1/2 red onion, chopped
3 cloves garlic, chopped
1 T. cayenne pepper
2 t. ground cumin

2 t. dried oregano
1 t. pepper
1/4 c. oil
taco shells
Garnish: favorite toppings

Place roast in a slow cooker; add water and set aside. In a blender, combine onion, garlic, spices and oil. Process until well mixed and pour over roast. Cover and cook on high setting for 6 to 7 hours, until roast is tender. Break roast apart with a fork. Reduce setting to low; cover and cook an additional hour. To serve, spoon into taco shells; garnish as desired. Serves 6 to 10.

For the easiest-ever get-together, host a bring-your-favorite-topping taco party. Just provide the shells and the slow-cooked beef or chicken...everyone else can bring lettuce, tomatoes, olives, shredded cheese, onion, salsa, sour cream and guacamole. Delicious!

Slow Cookers
to the Rescue

Mexican Chicken Soft Tacos

Shannon Hildebrandt
Saskatchewan, Canada

This tasty dish is oh-so simple. My brother-in-law Mike, who is a no-fuss cook, made this dish for my husband and me several years ago. It's been a big hit ever since...these are messy but good!

4 to 6 boneless, skinless
   chicken breasts
16-oz. jar chunky salsa
4-oz. can diced green chiles
1/2 onion, chopped
10-1/2 oz. pkg. 8 to 10-inch
   flour tortillas

Garnish: shredded lettuce, chopped tomatoes, sour cream, salsa, shredded Cheddar cheese

Place chicken in a slow cooker; top with salsa, chiles and onion. Cover and cook on low setting for 4 to 5 hours, until tender. Shred chicken using 2 forks. If desired, warm tortillas briefly in the microwave. To serve, fill each tortilla with 2 to 3 heaping tablespoons of chicken, being careful not to overfill. Top with remaining ingredients as desired. Fold tortillas over to make a taco, or roll like a burrito and fold in one end. Serves 4 to 6.

Jump-start tomorrow's dinner! Chop and assemble ingredients tonight, refrigerating meat and veggies in separate containers. In the morning, toss everything in the slow cooker...you're set to go!

Chuckwagon Chili

Lillian Child
Omaha, NE

I got this easy recipe from a co-worker many years ago and it's still the chili I return to over & over again. It has an excellent sweet flavor with a soupy consistency...this is not a thick chili. Serve with warm cornbread and a basket of saltine crackers...yum!

2 lbs. lean ground beef chuck
3 15-1/2 oz. cans chili beans
3 14-1/2 oz. cans stewed
  tomatoes
2 onions, chopped
2 green peppers, chopped

3 T. chili powder
salt and pepper to taste
Garnish: sour cream, shredded
  Cheddar cheese, sliced green
  onions

Place uncooked beef and remaining ingredients except garnish into a slow cooker in the order listed; stir once. Cover and cook on low setting for 8 to 10 hours, or on high setting for 6 to 8 hours. Garnish individual servings as desired. Makes 8 to 10 servings.

Stretch a pot of chili to feed lots more people...serve it Cincinnati-style! For 2-way chili, ladle chili over a bowl of spaghetti. For 3-way, top chili and spaghetti with shredded cheese. For 4-way, spoon diced onions on top of the cheese...add chili beans to the stack for 5-way. Scrumptious!

Yummy-Tummy Sausage Stew

Dina Willard
Abingdon, MD

My kids have declared this a new family hand-me-down recipe! I made up this stew one day when I was trying to use up some items in the pantry. My family loved it, and it will be a weeknight staple for years to come.

24-oz. jar marinara sauce, divided
2 to 3 lbs. sweet Italian pork sausage links, sliced 1/4-inch thick
16-oz. pkg. frozen stir-fry peppers and onions

16-oz. can white beans, drained
2 4-oz. cans sliced mushrooms, drained
Optional: 1/4 c. fresh basil, chopped
cooked rice

Pour half of the marinara sauce into a slow cooker; arrange uncooked sausage over sauce. In a bowl, combine frozen vegetables, beans, mushrooms and basil, if using. Spoon pepper mixture over sausage; pour remaining sauce on top. Cover and cook on low setting for 7 to 8 hours, until sausage is plump and cooked through. Serve stew over cooked rice. Makes 8 servings.

Mmm...freshly baked rolls, so cozy served with stew! Tie refrigerated bread stick dough into loose knots and arrange on a baking sheet. Brush with beaten egg and bake as package directs.

Chicken Veggie Soup

Alice Randall
Nacogdoches, TX

This recipe is a terrific way to use up leftover deli roast chicken. If your slow cooker isn't filled 2/3 full, you may add an extra can of veggies or noodle soup and a little more water. You can also use one can chicken noodle and one can cream of chicken soup. Delicious!

1-3/4 c. water, divided
1 to 2 c. cooked chicken,
   chopped or shredded
2 10-3/4 oz. cans chicken
   noodle soup

2 15-oz. cans no-salt-added
   mixed vegetables, drained
14-1/2 oz. can petite diced
   tomatoes
salt and pepper to taste

Add 1/2 cup water to a large slow cooker on high setting. Add chicken, soup, mixed vegetables and tomatoes with juice. Stir; add remaining water. Cover and cook on high setting for 3 hours. Before serving, add salt and pepper to taste. Serves 6.

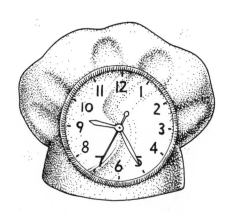

Do you have a favorite family stovetop soup recipe that you don't serve often due to lack of time? Try making it in a slow cooker instead! A recipe that simmers for 2 hours on the stovetop can generally cook all day on the low setting without overcooking.

Taco Chicken Soup

Jackie Flood
Geneseo, NY

*This soup is very satisfying and so easy to prepare! Substitute a
can of baked beans for the refried beans, if you like.*

2 boneless, skinless chicken
  breasts
15-1/2 oz. can kidney beans,
  drained and rinsed
15-1/2 oz. black beans, drained
  and rinsed

16-oz. can fat-free refried beans
15-1/2 oz. diced tomatoes, plain
  or with green chiles
1-1/4 oz. pkg. taco seasoning
  mix
15-1/4 oz. can corn, drained

Place chicken in a slow cooker; add beans and tomatoes with juice.
Sprinkle with taco seasoning; stir to mix in. Cover and cook on low
setting for 6 to 8 hours. Remove chicken and shred with 2 forks.
Return chicken to slow cooker along with corn. Cover and cook on
low setting an additional 20 to 30 minutes, until warmed through.
Serves 4 to 6.

A fast & fun new way to serve cornbread! Mix up the batter,
thin slightly with a little extra milk, then bake until
crisp in a waffle iron.

Poor Man's Beef Stew

Susan Wilson
Johnson City, TN

My mom often made this simple stew for our family, especially during the winter months, with hot buttery cornbread. We always enjoyed it so much...I still do!

6 potatoes, peeled and quartered
3 carrots, peeled and diced
1 onion, coarsely chopped
salt and pepper to taste

1 lb. ground beef, browned
    and drained
10-3/4 oz. can tomato soup

Layer vegetables in a slow cooker; add salt and pepper to taste. Crumble browned beef on top; spread soup over beef. Cover and cook on low setting for 6 hours, or on high setting for 4 hours. Makes 6 servings.

Hearty Minestrone

Amy Butcher
Columbus, GA

So yummy and so easy!

1/2 lb. sweet Italian ground
    pork sausage, browned and
    drained
14-1/2 oz. can Italian-style
    diced tomatoes
1.35-oz. pkg. onion soup mix
15-1/2 oz. can cannellini beans,
    drained and rinsed

15-1/2 oz. can pinto beans,
    drained and rinsed
2-1/2 c. water
1 c. carrots, peeled and sliced
1 c. celery, sliced
Garnish: shredded Parmesan
    cheese

In a slow cooker, combine sausage, tomatoes in juice and remaining ingredients except cheese. Cover and cook on low setting for 8 to 10 hours, or on high setting for 4 to 6 hours. Garnish with cheese. Makes 8 servings.

Keep grocery lists and refrigerator artwork hanging in style!
Use hot glue to attach magnets to game pieces...dominoes
and checkers are fun.

Ham & Potato Soup

Tiffany Burdette
Everson, WA

After a big family Easter dinner, there was so much ham left, I didn't know what to do with it! This satisfying soup recipe was just right. Save room for seconds, because you'll definitely want more! This soup freezes and reheats really well.

3-1/2 c. potatoes, peeled and
   diced
1/3 c. celery, chopped
1/3 c. onion, finely chopped
3/4 c. cooked ham, diced
3-1/4 c. water

6 cubes chicken bouillon
1/2 t. salt
1 t. pepper
5 T. butter
5 T. all-purpose flour
2 c. milk

In a slow cooker, combine all ingredients except butter, flour and milk. Cover and cook on low setting for 6 to 8 hours, until potatoes are fork-tender. About 20 minutes before serving, melt butter in a saucepan over medium heat; stir in flour. Gradually add milk, stirring constantly until thickened. Stir mixture into soup in slow cooker. Cover and cook on low setting an additional 15 to 20 minutes, until thickened. Makes 8 servings.

If you enjoy creamy soups, try substituting canned evaporated milk for half-and-half or whole milk. It holds up well in slow-cooker recipes, doesn't need refrigeration and is lower in fat too.

Savory Red Cabbage & Apples

Carol Lytle
Columbus, OH

*I love to serve this dish alongside bratwurst and German potato salad...
all the fun and flavor of Oktoberfest served up in a jiffy!*

1 head red cabbage, coarsely
   sliced
2 onions, coarsely chopped
6 tart apples, cored and
   quartered
2 t. salt

2 c. hot water
3 T. sugar
2/3 c. cider vinegar
1/3 c. bacon drippings or butter,
   melted

Place cabbage, onions and apples in a slow cooker; sprinkle with salt.
Combine remaining ingredients; pour over cabbage mixture. Cover
and cook on low setting for 8 to 10 hours. Stir well and serve. Makes
about 6 servings.

Make family dinners memorable! It's easy to tote along a
picnic supper. Eat in the backyard, or even pack up dinner
and go to a nearby park.

Spanish Rice

Elizabeth Blackstone
Racine, WI

*It's terrific to get home and find dinner all ready in my slow cooker!
Sometimes I'll add a pound of browned ground beef
to this recipe to make it a main dish.*

15-1/2 oz. can diced tomatoes
15-oz. can tomato sauce
1 onion, diced
1 green pepper, chopped
2 cloves garlic, minced
1-1/2 c. water

2 T. chunky salsa
2 t. chili powder
1 t. ground cumin
3/4 c. long-cooking rice,
   uncooked

Mix together undrained tomatoes and remaining ingredients in a slow cooker. Cover and cook on low setting for 7 to 8 hours, until rice is tender. Makes 4 to 6 servings.

It's not how much we have, but how much
we enjoy, that makes happiness.
– Charles Haddon-Spurgeon

Cheesy Scalloped Potatoes

Brittney Winters
Ontario, Canada

We like scalloped potatoes. None of the recipes I found were exactly what I was looking for, so I decided to create my own. We absolutely love this creamy, cheesy recipe. Serve with baked ham and enjoy!

10-3/4 oz. can Cheddar cheese
  soup
10-3/4 oz. can cream of broccoli
  soup
1-1/4 c. milk
2 c. Swiss cheese, cut into strips

1 yellow onion, diced
2 cloves garlic, minced
6 to 8 potatoes, peeled and
  thinly sliced
3 c. shredded Cheddar cheese
4 green onions, chopped

In a bowl, mix soups, milk, Swiss cheese, yellow onion and garlic; set aside. Spray a slow cooker with non-stick vegetable spray. Layer some of the potatoes, soup mixture, Cheddar cheese and green onions. Repeat layering until all of the ingredients have been used. Cover and cook on low setting for 8 to 10 hours, or on high setting for 5 to 6 hours. Serves 6 to 8.

Creamy Polenta

Mia Rossi
Charlotte, NC

I like to serve my favorite hearty pasta sauce over polenta as a change from spaghetti. This is such an easy no-fuss way to fix polenta...there's no need to stand over a hot stove stirring!

6 c. boiling water
2 T. butter, sliced
2 t. salt

1 t. pepper
2 c. cornmeal
1 c. grated Parmesan cheese

In a slow cooker sprayed with non-stick vegetable spray, combine boiling water, butter, salt and pepper. Add cornmeal gradually; whisk until smooth. Cover and cook on low setting for 6 to 8 hours. At serving time, stir in cheese. Makes 6 to 8 servings.

Slow Cookers
to the Rescue

Slow-Cooked Pierogies

Sherry Gordon
Arlington Heights, IL

*These buttery pierogies are yummy with a steamed green veggie.
Frozen pierogies come in lots of different flavors...I keep several
tucked in the freezer to go with whatever else is on the menu.*

2 16-oz. pkgs. frozen potato
    and cheese pierogies
1/2 c. butter, sliced

1/2 to 1 onion, chopped
salt and pepper to taste

Place frozen pierogies in a lightly greased slow cooker; set aside. Melt
butter in a skillet over medium heat; cook onion until golden. Spoon
mixture over pierogies; add salt and pepper to taste. Cover and cook
on high setting for 3 hours. Turn pierogies with tongs twice during
cooking time to coat with butter mixture. Serves 8.

Children are sure to be helpful in the kitchen when they're wearing
their very own kid-size aprons. Visit a craft store to select plain
canvas aprons and fabric crayons, then let kids decorate their
apron as they like. Follow package directions for
making the design permanent. So sweet!

Farmstand Veggie Roast

Jill Burton
Gooseberry Patch

After we've been to the farmers' market, I love to make this savory mix of fresh vegetables. It's delicious all by itself or stirred into pasta for a meatless meal.

1 lb. baby carrots
1 onion, cut into wedges
1/3 c. olive oil
2 t. Italian seasoning
1 t. garlic, minced
1 t. salt
1/4 t. pepper
1/2 t. sugar

2-1/2 c. cauliflower, cut into flowerets
1 zucchini, sliced 1/4-inch thick
1 yellow squash, sliced 1/4-inch thick
1-1/2 c. asparagus, cut into 1-inch pieces

Place carrots and onion in a large slow cooker; set aside. In a small bowl, mix olive oil and seasonings. Pour half of oil mixture into slow cooker; toss to coat. Cover and cook on high setting for 2 to 2-1/2 hours, until tender. Toss remaining oil mixture and remaining vegetables together; add to slow cooker. Cover and cook on high setting an additional 30 to 45 minutes, until crisp-tender. Makes 6 to 8 servings.

Slow-roasted vegetables are flavorful, nutritious and so versatile. Serve them warm as a side dish, or let cool and spoon over crisp greens, drizzled with vinaigrette dressing, for a tasty salad. They can even be tossed with thin spaghetti and crumbled feta cheese for a hearty meatless main dish.

All-Day Ratatoûille

Cathy Hillier
Salt Lake City, UT

*After we went to see the movie of the same name, my kids were so
excited to find out we could actually make ratatoûille at home! Who
knew a cartoon mouse could get kids to eat their vegetables?*

1 onion, diced
2 T. olive oil
3 cloves garlic, minced
28-oz. can stewed tomatoes
1 eggplant, peeled and cubed
1 zucchini, halved lengthwise
   and thinly sliced

1 yellow squash, halved
   lengthwise and thinly sliced
1 green pepper, diced
1 T. fresh thyme, chopped
1 T. fresh oregano, chopped
salt and pepper to taste

In a skillet over medium heat, sauté onion in oil until soft. Add garlic;
sauté for one minute and remove from heat. Combine undrained
tomatoes and remaining ingredients in a slow cooker. Add onion
mixture; stir gently. Cover and cook on low setting for 5 to 6 hours.
Serves 6 to 8.

Once a week, take it easy and have a leftovers night! Set out
leftovers so everyone can choose their favorite. End with
scoops of ice cream for dessert...what could be simpler?

Molasses Baked Beans

Robin Cornett
Pryor, OK

This is always a hit for summer meals...you don't have to turn on your stove and heat up the kitchen!

1 meaty ham hock or ham bone
16-oz. pkg. dried white beans,
    rinsed
3 to 3-1/2 c. water
1/3 c. molasses

1/4 c. brown sugar, packed
1 onion, finely chopped
1 T. mustard
1/2 t. salt

Place all ingredients in a slow cooker in order given; stir gently. Cover and cook on high setting for 7 to 8 hours, until beans are tender. Remove ham bone; cool. Cut ham from bone and stir into beans; discard bone. Makes 6 to 8 servings.

Mama's Spicy Beans

Yvette Garza
Livingston, CA

My family and I love beans. I make these often...so simple!

10 c. water
5 c. dried pinto beans, rinsed
2 T. bacon drippings
1 T. salt

2 1.35-oz. pkgs. onion soup
    mix
1 T. chili powder
paprika and pepper to taste

Combine water, beans and bacon drippings in a slow cooker. Cover and cook on high setting for 4 to 6 hours, until beans begin to split. Stir in remaining ingredients. Cover and cook on high setting an additional 2 hours. Serves 10.

Iced tea is refreshing anytime! Simply place 2 family-size teabags in a 2-quart pitcher of cold water. Refrigerate overnight to brew. Sweeten to taste and serve over ice.

Soup's On!

Tom's Chili Con Carne

Catherine Reynolds
Scottsdale, AZ

My dad used to make this chili for us every winter. It's the only time he ever cooked. Daddy called the green pepper a "mango" for reasons he never made clear, even though we told him a mango was something entirely different! Little did we know that that's what some folks used to call green peppers back in Dayton, Ohio, where Dad grew up. This chili is terrific with cornmeal muffins!

1 lb. ground beef
1 onion, diced
1 green pepper, diced
15-oz. can plain or seasoned
   diced tomatoes
15-oz. can dark red kidney
   beans

1/2 c. water
2 T. vinegar
1 T. sugar
salt and pepper to taste

Brown beef and onion together in a large skillet over medium heat; drain. Add green pepper, undrained tomatoes and beans, water, vinegar and sugar, stirring after each addition. Reduce heat and simmer for about 30 minutes, stirring occasionally. Individual servings may be seasoned to taste with salt and pepper. Makes 5 to 6 servings.

Watch tag sales for a big red speckled enamelware stockpot... it's just the right size for cooking up a family-size batch of soup. The bright color adds a homey touch to any soup supper!

Red, White & Green Chili

Diane Cohen
The Woodlands, TX

*Dollop bowls of this hearty chili with sour cream and
serve with crisp white tortilla chips...delicious!*

1 lb. lean ground beef
1 onion, chopped
1 t. garlic, chopped
15-oz. can diced tomatoes
2 15-oz. cans Great Northern
    beans, drained and rinsed

16-oz. jar green salsa
14-oz. can chicken broth
1-1/2 t. ground cumin
2 T. fresh cilantro, chopped

In a Dutch oven over medium heat, cook beef and onion until no
longer pink; drain. Add garlic, tomatoes with juice and remaining
ingredients except cilantro. Bring to a boil; reduce heat. Cover and
simmer for 15 minutes. At serving time, stir one tablespoon cilantro
into chili. Sprinkle remaining cilantro over each bowl of chili.
Serves 4.

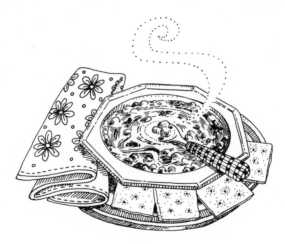

An easy way to thicken a pot of chili and add scrumptious
corn flavor too. Combine 1/2 cup water and 1/4 cup masa harina flour
(from the Mexican food aisle). Add to a simmering pot of chili,
stir until smooth and cook until warmed through.

Escarole & Rice Soup

Heidi Thullen
Manorville, NY

My mom, who is in her eighties, gave me this recipe years ago. I've been making it for at least twenty years and sometimes bring it to work to share with others. Enjoy with a loaf of fresh-baked bread.

1 lb. escarole, leaves separated
   and well rinsed
3 T. olive oil
1 onion, chopped
2 t. garlic, finely chopped
salt to taste

5 c. chicken broth, divided
1/2 c. long-cooking white or
   brown rice, uncooked
pepper to taste
Garnish: shredded Parmesan
   cheese

Stack escarole leaves and slice into one-inch strips; set aside. Heat oil in a heavy soup kettle over medium heat. Sauté onion and garlic until golden, about 3 minutes. Add escarole and sprinkle lightly with salt; cook for 3 minutes. Add one cup broth. Reduce heat to low; cover and cook until escarole is tender, about 15 minutes. Add remaining broth; increase heat to medium-high and bring to a boil. Stir in uncooked rice; reduce heat. Cover and simmer for about 12 minutes, until rice is tender but still firm. Add more salt and pepper as desired. Sprinkle with cheese just before serving. Makes 5 to 6 servings.

Take time to share family stories
and traditions with your kids!
A cherished family recipe can be
a great conversation starter
at dinner.

Soup's On!

Hearty Healthy Minestrone

Kristen DeSimone
Peabody, MA

I love to make homemade soups with the freshest ingredients possible.
This satisfying meatless soup has proven to be a big hit with my family.
Serve with a side of crusty garlic bread...yum!

1 to 2 T. olive oil
1 onion, diced
3 to 4 cloves garlic, minced
2 to 3 carrots, peeled and diced
32-oz. container vegetable broth
2 15-1/2 oz. cans diced
   tomatoes
15-1/2 oz. can cannellini beans
1 zucchini, diced
fresh basil to taste, coarsely
   chopped

1 t. Italian seasoning
sea salt and pepper to taste
1/3 c. elbow macaroni,
   uncooked
1 bunch baby spinach, torn
hot pepper sauce to taste
Garnish: shredded Parmesan
   cheese

Heat oil in a large soup pot over medium-high heat. Add onion, garlic
and carrots. Sauté about 5 minutes, until onion is translucent. Add
broth, undrained tomatoes and beans, zucchini, basil and seasonings.
Reduce heat to low; cover and simmer for 10 minutes. Stir in
uncooked macaroni. Simmer, covered, an additional 10 minutes,
stirring occasionally. Add spinach, hot pepper sauce and more salt and
pepper to taste. Simmer, covered, about 20 minutes more. Serve with
a sprinkling of cheese. Makes about 6 servings.

Use a potato peeler to quickly cut thin curls of cheese
for garnishing soup, salad or pasta.

Greek Chicken & Rice Soup

Dawn Henning
Gooseberry Patch

Whenever I serve a rotisserie chicken with rice for supper, I know I'll be enjoying this zingy, easy-to-fix soup the next night. Pita bread and marinated tomatoes go well with it.

4 c. chicken broth
2 c. cooked rice, warmed and
   divided
2 egg yolks, beaten
3 T. lemon juice
1 T. lemon zest

1 to 2 c. deli roast chicken,
   shredded
salt and pepper to taste
Optional: 2 T. fresh dill or
   parsley, chopped

In a large saucepan over medium heat, bring broth to a simmer. Transfer one cup hot broth to a blender. Add 1/2 cup cooked rice, egg yolks, lemon juice and zest to blender; process until smooth. Stir rice mixture into simmering broth; add chicken and remaining rice. Simmer, stirring frequently, until slightly thickened, about 10 minutes. Add salt and pepper to taste. At serving time, stir in dill or parsley, if desired. Makes 4 servings.

For a speedy Greek salad that can be made any time of year, combine quartered roma tomatoes with sliced black olives, crumbled feta cheese and chopped red onion. Drizzle with Italian salad dressing and toss to mix.

Soup's On!

Sausage Bean Gumbo

Jo Cline
Smithville, MO

Quick & easy...ready in thirty minutes!

1 lb. smoked pork sausage link,
  sliced
3 15-1/2 oz. cans Great
  Northern beans
 15-1/2 oz. can diced tomatoes
  with sweet onions

1 stalk celery, diced
1/2 c. green pepper, diced
1/2 t. garlic powder
1/4 t. pepper
Optional: fresh cilantro, chopped

In a large saucepan over low heat, combine all ingredients except
garnish; do not drain vegetables. Cover and simmer for about
30 minutes, stirring occasionally. Sprinkle servings with cilantro, if
desired. Makes 4 servings.

Keep fast-cooking ramen noodles on hand for quick meals.
Make a comforting chicken noodle soup by stirring in
shredded chicken and diced veggies or simply top drained
noodles with pasta sauce or gravy. Speedy!

Y'all Luv It Veggie Soup

Tracy Whited
Dayton, OH

Every autumn, my husband and I love to take long drives in the countryside to see all the farmers harvesting their crops. This soup is our favorite meal after seeing the beautiful bounty of Mother Nature. My sister & brother say it's great for football weekends too. It freezes very well for a quick warm-up on busy weekdays.

1-1/2 lbs. ground beef
46-oz. can cocktail vegetable
  juice
16-oz. pkg. frozen mixed
  vegetables
2 potatoes, peeled and cubed

2 c. water
4 cubes beef bouillon
3 T. Worcestershire sauce
1 t. browning and seasoning
  sauce

In a stockpot over medium heat, brown beef. Drain; rinse beef with warm water and return to stockpot. Add remaining ingredients. Cover and simmer until vegetables are tender, stirring occasionally, about 30 minutes. Makes 6 to 8 servings.

Not enough soup bowls on hand for family & friends? Open the cupboards and pull out sturdy mugs! They're just as nice, and the handles make them easy to hold.

Stuffed Green Pepper Soup

Barb Rudyk
Alberta, Canada

This is a comforting soup for a cold day. Its flavor gets even better the day after...a terrific make-ahead dinner! Serve with cornbread or another hearty bread.

1/2 lb. ground beef	14-1/2 oz. can diced tomatoes
2 c. green pepper, chopped	10-3/4 oz. can tomato soup
1 c. onion, chopped	1/4 t. pepper
14-oz. can beef broth	1-1/2 c. cooked rice, warmed

Brown beef in a Dutch oven over medium-high heat; drain. Add green pepper and onion; cook about 8 minutes, until vegetables are just tender. Stir in broth, undrained tomatoes, soup and pepper; bring to a boil. Reduce heat to low; cover and simmer 45 minutes, stirring occasionally. To serve, divide cooked rice among 6 soup bowls; ladle soup over rice. Makes 6 servings.

Be a savvy shopper. Make a shopping list, grouping items by the area of the store where they're found...produce, meats, canned goods and frozen foods. You'll breeze right down the aisles.

Debbie's Foolproof Potato Soup

Candi Fisher
Gallipolis, OH

I never had good luck with potato soup...I always ended up with something more like mashed potatoes. My mother-in-law shared this recipe with me and it was a success!

8 potatoes, peeled and chopped
1/2 to 1 onion, diced
10-3/4 oz. can cream of celery
  soup

3 to 4 T. butter, sliced
1/2 c. shredded Cheddar cheese
1 T. garlic powder, or to taste
2 to 3 c. milk

Place potatoes and onion in a large pot; add enough water to just cover. Bring to a boil over medium-high heat. Cook until vegetables are tender, about 15 to 20 minutes. Do not drain. Stir in soup; reduce heat and simmer for several minutes. Stir in butter; add cheese, garlic powder and milk to desired thickness. Cover; simmer over low heat for 15 to 20 minutes, stirring frequently. Serves 6.

Mom's Classic Potato Soup

Melissa Huddlestun
Nampa, ID

My mom used to make this potato soup all the time, especially on chilly days. Pass the crackers, please!

6 to 7 russet potatoes, peeled
  and diced
10-3/4 oz. can cream of celery
  soup
2-1/2 c. milk

2 t. celery salt
16-oz. pkg. shredded sharp
  Cheddar cheese
pepper to taste

In a large saucepan, cover potatoes with water. Bring to a boil over medium-high heat. Cook until potatoes are tender, about 15 to 20 minutes. Drain half of the cooking water; stir in remaining ingredients. Reduce heat to low. Cook, stirring occasionally, until cheese is melted and soup is heated through. Makes 6 servings.

Soup's On!

Chicken Corn Chowder

Linda Bair
Jeffersonville, OH

This is a terrific feel-good recipe for when you come home from a busy day at work. I serve it with warm cornbread and iced tea.

3 c. water
32-oz. pkg. frozen diced
   potatoes
32-oz. pkg. frozen corn
1/4 c. carrot, peeled and grated
2 T. celery, diced
1 T. dried, chopped onion
1 c. cooked chicken, diced

salt and pepper to taste
6 slices bacon, crisply cooked
   and crumbled
5-oz. can evaporated milk
1 c. half-and-half
Optional: 1/2 c. instant mashed
   potato flakes

In a large soup kettle over medium-high heat, combine water, vegetables, chicken, salt and pepper. Bring to a boil. Reduce heat; cover and simmer 15 minutes, or until potatoes are tender. Add bacon, milk and half-and-half; heat through. If chowder is too thin, stir in potato flakes to desired consistency. Makes 6 to 8 servings.

Quick Corn Chowder

Beth Bennett
Stratham, NH

When we came home from school on a snowy day, Mother would have this soup simmering on the stove. It filled the house with such a wonderful aroma and always warmed us through & through.

1/2 c. onion, chopped
1 T. bacon drippings or oil
10-3/4 oz. can cream of
   mushroom soup

2-1/2 c. creamed corn
4 c. milk
Optional: 4 hot dogs, sliced

In a large saucepan over medium heat, cook onion in drippings or oil until tender; drain. Add remaining ingredients; reduce heat to low. Cover and simmer for 15 to 20 minutes, stirring frequently. Serves 4.

Seafood Chowder

Roberta Simpkins
Mentor on the Lake, OH

I found this recipe in an old cookbook I bought at a book sale at our local library! I usually make biscuits to serve with it. If company is coming, I like to add some crabmeat and asparagus to the chowder.

1 t. oil
1 c. onion, chopped
1/2 t. garlic powder
10-3/4 oz. can cream of celery
    soup
10-3/4 oz. can of cream of
    potato soup

1-3/4 c. milk
1/2 lb. peeled medium shrimp
1/2 lb. firm white fish fillet,
    cubed
1 t. fresh dill, chopped

Heat oil in a large saucepan over medium heat; add onion and garlic powder. Cook until onion is tender; drain. Stir in soups and milk. Heat to a boil, stirring often. Add shrimp and fish. Cook over low heat for about 5 minutes, stirring occasionally, until shrimp turns pink and fish flakes easily. Stir in dill just before serving. Makes 4 servings.

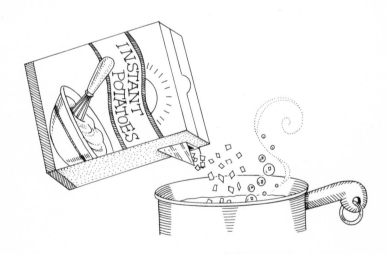

If a pot of soup is too thin, thicken it with just a sprinkling of instant mashed potato flakes. Works every time!

Soup's On!

Hearty Shrimp Chowder

Susan Lacy
Vancouver, WA

*This rich-tasting chowder is often served at our family gatherings,
especially in the winter. Sliced carrots and frozen corn
are good additions.*

2 c. potatoes, peeled and diced
1/2 c. onion, chopped
1 to 2 c. boiling water
1 cube chicken bouillon
2 c. peeled medium shrimp
1/4 c. margarine, melted

1/3 c. all-purpose flour
1/2 t. salt
pepper to taste
1/4 t. dried thyme
4 c. milk, heated just to boiling

In a large saucepan, combine potatoes, onion, boiling water and
bouillon cube. Cook over medium-high heat until potatoes are tender,
10 to 15 minutes; do not drain. Reduce heat to low; add shrimp. In a
small bowl, blend melted margarine and flour together; stir into
chowder and continue simmering. As chowder thickens, stir in
remaining ingredients. Simmer, stirring occasionally, until heated
through. Makes 6 servings.

Keep frozen shrimp on hand for delicious meals anytime. Let it
thaw overnight in the fridge, or for a quicker way, place the
frozen shrimp in a colander and run ice-cold water over it.
Don't thaw shrimp in the microwave, as it will get mushy.

Zesty Mexican Noodle Soup

Tiffany Jones
Locust Grove, AR

This yummy soup is great to savor on a cold rainy night while watching a favorite movie. I like to serve Mexican cornbread with it.

4 14-1/2 oz. cans beef broth
14-1/2 oz. can diced tomatoes
   with green chiles
15-1/2 oz. can black beans,
   drained and rinsed
15-1/2 oz. can light red kidney
   beans, drained and rinsed

15-1/4 oz. can corn, drained
1-1/4 oz. pkg. taco seasoning
   mix
1-oz. pkg. ranch salad dressing
   mix
12-oz. pkg. wide egg noodles,
   uncooked

Combine broth, undrained tomatoes and remaining ingredients except noodles in a large soup pot. Bring to a boil over medium heat. Stir in uncooked noodles; reduce heat slightly and simmer 20 to 25 minutes, stirring occasionally, until noodles are tender. Makes 8 servings.

Freeze leftover soup in individual portions to serve later as a soup buffet supper...everyone can choose their favorite! Just add a basket of warm buttered rolls for a cozy, quick & easy meal.

Soup's On!

Texas Taco Soup

Denise Bennett
Anderson, IN

A neighbor who moved here from Texas shared this very hearty soup recipe. It's a nice alternative to chili...even our picky seven-year-old son loves it! Tomato juice can be added if you like a thinner consistency. This tastes even better the next day, if there's any left!

1 lb. ground beef
1/2 onion, diced
19-oz. can mild or hot chili
   beans
14-1/2 oz. can diced tomatoes
   with green chiles
1-oz. pkg. spicy ranch salad
   dressing mix

14-oz. can black beans, drained
14-3/4 oz. can shoepeg corn,
   drained
Garnish: tortilla strips, sour
   cream, shredded Cheddar
   cheese, diced green onions,
   sliced avocado

In a stockpot over medium heat, brown beef with onion; drain. Stir in undrained chili beans and tomatoes; add remaining ingredients. Reduce heat to low; cover and simmer for 30 minutes. Ladle into bowls and garnish as desired. Serves 6 to 8.

Write or paste your most-used recipes on 4"x6" index cards...they'll fit perfectly into a flip photo album. The plastic pages will protect your recipes from spatters and you'll save time finding the recipe you need.

Creamy Chicken Noodle Soup

Kathy Landes
Wooster, OH

This soup disappears quickly with requests for more! It's quick & easy to prepare and can easily be doubled.

4 c. water
4 cubes chicken bouillon
3 c. medium egg noodles, uncooked
Optional: 1/4 c. carrot, peeled and chopped, and 1/4 c. celery, chopped

10-3/4 oz. can cream of chicken soup
1-1/2 c. cooked chicken, cubed
1/2 c. sour cream
1/2 t. dried parsley

In a large saucepan over medium-high heat, bring water and bouillon cubes to a boil. Add uncooked noodles with carrot and celery, if using. Boil, uncovered, until noodles are tender, about 10 to 12 minutes. Do not drain. Stir in soup and chicken; reduce heat to low and heat through. Remove from heat; stir in sour cream. Sprinkle with parsley before serving. Makes 6 to 8 servings.

Soup is so nice when shared. Thank a friend with a basket of warm rolls and a pot of steaming homemade soup. What a welcome surprise on a brisk day!

Granny's Vegetable Soup

Kimberly Freeman
Mountain Grove, MO

My sister and I always request this soup when we visit our Granny and Papa. It's easy to make it go farther by adding extra veggies. This is one of my most treasured recipes from Granny.

1/2 to 1 lb. ground beef
3 to 4 potatoes, peeled and chopped
2 8-oz. cans tomato sauce
16-oz. pkg. frozen mixed vegetables

15-1/2 oz. can kidney or pinto beans, drained
8-oz. can sliced water chestnuts, drained
1/4 t. onion salt
1/4 t. sugar

Brown beef in a large saucepan over medium heat; drain. Add remaining ingredients; reduce heat to low. Cover and cook about 30 minutes, stirring occasionally, until vegetables are tender. Makes 6 to 8 servings.

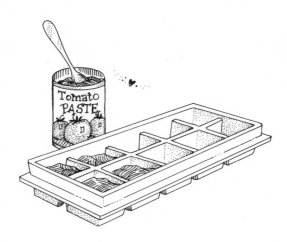

A spoonful of tomato paste adds rich flavor to stews and roasts. If you have a partial can left over, freeze the rest in ice cube trays, then pop out and store in a freezer bag.

Chicken & Broccoli Soup

Barbara Kinser
Brentwood, TN

Hearty and filling! Use fresh chopped broccoli if you wish.

6-oz. pkg. long-grain and
    wild rice
32-oz. container chicken broth
16-oz. pkg. frozen broccoli,
    thawed and drained

3-lb. deli roast chicken,
    shredded
8-oz. pkg. cream cheese, cubed
    and softened

In a soup pot, cook rice according to package directions. Add broth, broccoli and chicken. Bring to a boil over medium heat. Reduce heat to low. Cover and simmer for 15 to 20 minutes. Stir in cream cheese; simmer for a few minutes, until heated through. Serves 8.

Katie's 8-Can Soup

Katie Majeske
Denver, PA

So easy and so good! The seasoning in the cans of chili is all you need to make this soup taste delicious. Add some crusty bread and your dinner is complete!

15-1/2 oz. can chili with beans
15-1/2 oz. can chili without
    beans

6 15-oz. cans assorted favorite
    vegetables

In a stockpot over medium heat, combine all ingredients. Do not drain any of the cans. Cover and simmer until heated through, stirring occasionally, 15 to 20 minutes. Makes 10 to 12 servings.

Stir some alphabet pasta into
a pot of vegetable soup...the kids
will love it!

Soup's On!

Sausage Soup Florentine

Lisa LaGaipa
Fairfield, CT

I've been making this quick go-to soup for years. I often serve it with some stuffed bread for a light yet satisfying simple dinner.

1/2 lb. sweet Italian ground or
   link pork sausage
2 c. chicken broth
14-1/2 oz. can seasoned diced
   tomatoes
1/2 c. small soup pasta,
   uncooked

salt and pepper to taste
2 c. spinach, chopped
Optional: grated Parmesan
   cheese

Remove sausage from casings, if using links. In a large saucepan over medium heat, brown and crumble sausage; drain. Add broth, undrained tomatoes and uncooked pasta; bring to a boil over high heat. Reduce heat; cover and simmer 10 minutes, or until pasta is tender. Remove from heat; season to taste with salt and pepper. Add spinach; stir until wilted. If desired, sprinkle with cheese. Serves 4.

Turn leftover hamburger buns into slices of garlic bread in a jiffy!
Spread with softened butter, sprinkle with garlic salt and
broil until toasty and golden...yum!

Tony's Peasant Soup

Linda Cuellar
Riverside, CA

My husband isn't a big fan of soup, but he does love this one!
Serve with crusty Italian bread.

1 T. olive oil
1 lb. sweet Italian pork
   sausage links, cut into
   1/2-inch slices
1/2 lb. boneless, skinless
   chicken breast, cut into
   1/2-inch cubes
3/4 c. onion, chopped
1/2 t. garlic, minced
14-1/2 oz. can chicken broth

14-1/2 oz. can diced tomatoes
   with basil, garlic and
   oregano
15-oz. can cannellini beans,
   drained
Optional: 1/2 t. red pepper
   flakes
1 c. fresh basil, chopped
Garnish: grated Parmesan
   cheese

Heat oil in a large heavy saucepan over medium heat. Cook sausage and chicken until no longer pink. Add onion and garlic; cook until soft and translucent. Drain; add broth, undrained tomatoes, beans and red pepper flakes, if using. Bring to a boil. Reduce heat to low; cover and simmer for 15 to 20 minutes. Stir in basil and cook for another 10 minutes. Ladle into bowls and sprinkle with cheese. Serves 4 to 6.

A toasty touch for soups! Butter bread slices and cut into shapes using mini cookie cutters. Heat on a baking sheet at 425 degrees until crisp and then garnish filled soup bowls before serving.

Soup's On!

Meatballs & Pasta Soup

Gloria Kaufmann
Orrville, OH

*A hearty favorite of our family. Use your own homemade meatballs,
if you like...you'll need about thirty. This soup freezes well.*

1 c. spiral or shell pasta,
  uncooked
28-oz. can diced tomatoes
2 14-1/2 oz. cans chicken broth
14-oz. jar meatless spaghetti
  sauce
1-1/2 c. frozen sliced carrots,
  thawed

16-oz. pkg. frozen meatballs,
  thawed
16-oz. can kidney beans,
  drained and rinsed
4-1/2 oz. can sliced mushrooms,
  drained
1 c. frozen peas

Cook pasta according to package directions; drain. While pasta is
cooking, combine undrained tomatoes and remaining ingredients in a
soup kettle. Bring to a boil over medium heat, stirring occasionally.
Reduce heat; cover and simmer for 5 minutes. Add cooked pasta to
soup; heat through. Makes 10 servings.

To get rid of an onion smell after slicing, simply hold
your hands under cold running water along with a
stainless steel spoon or other utensil.

Tomato Tortellini Soup

Emily Hartzell
Portland, IN

Easy and so tasty! Keep the ingredients on hand and you'll be able to stir up a pot of soup in just minutes.

2 cloves garlic, minced
1 T. olive oil
2 14-1/2 oz. cans chicken broth
2 14-1/2 oz. cans diced
  tomatoes

9-oz. pkg. refrigerated cheese
  tortellini
1 T. fresh basil, chopped, or
  1 t. dried basil
salt and pepper to taste

In a large saucepan over medium heat, cook garlic in oil until fragrant. Stir in broth and undrained tomatoes; bring to a boil. Add tortellini. Reduce heat and simmer for about 10 minutes, until tortellini is tender. Stir in basil; season with salt and pepper. Makes 4 to 6 servings.

Quesadillas are quick and filling partners for a bowl of soup...a nice change from grilled cheese too! Sprinkle a flour tortilla with shredded cheese, top with another tortilla and microwave on high until the cheese melts. Cut into wedges and serve with salsa.

Soup's On!

Cheesy Black Bean Soup

Delania Owen
Jonesboro, AR

Whenever I need a hot meal fast, this is the tried & true recipe I choose...yum!

15-1/2 oz. can black beans, drained
15-1/4 oz. can corn
15-1/2 oz. can diced tomatoes with green chiles and cilantro
1 t. garlic powder

1 t. chili powder
1/2 t. ground cumin
1/2 to 1 lb. pasteurized process cheese, cubed
Garnish: sour cream, corn chips

Combine beans and undrained corn and tomatoes in a stockpot over medium-low heat; stir. Add seasonings and cheese. Cover and simmer until heated through and cheese is melted. Serve with sour cream and corn chips. Makes 6 to 8 servings.

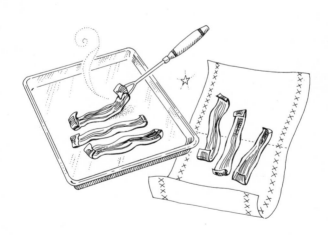

Crumbled bacon is a tasty garnish on bowls of soup, and here's an easy way to make it. Arrange bacon slices on a rimmed baking sheet and bake at 350 degrees. They'll be crispy in about 15 minutes...no messy spatters!

Julie's Hamburger Soup

Julie Bell
Fruit Heights, UT

Our family has enjoyed this simple soup recipe for years. For the best flavor ever, I especially like to use home-canned tomato juice.

1 lb. ground beef
1 onion, chopped
1 c. water
2 c. carrots, peeled and grated
1/4 t. garlic salt
1/4 t. salt

1/4 t. pepper
1 bay leaf
3 c. tomato juice
2 10-3/4 oz. cans cream of
   celery soup

In a large saucepan over medium heat, brown beef and onion; drain. Add water, carrots and seasonings. Reduce heat to low. Cover and simmer for 30 minutes, stirring occasionally. Stir in tomato juice and soup. Simmer until heated through. Discard bay leaf before serving. Serves 6 to 8.

Need to add a little zing to a pot of soup? Just add
a splash of Worcestershire sauce, lemon juice
or flavored vinegar.

Beef Noodle Soup

Kathy Walstrom
Glenview, IL

*Homestyle frozen noodles add so much to this soup! I always double
this recipe and freeze what's left over for another day.*

1 to 2 T. oil
1 lb. stew beef, cubed
1 c. onion, chopped
1 c. celery, chopped
5-3/4 c. water
1/4 c. beef soup base
1 c. carrots, peeled and chopped

14-1/2 oz. can green beans,
  partially drained
1/4 t. dried parsley
1/8 t. pepper
2-1/2 c. frozen egg noodles,
  uncooked

Heat oil in a stockpot over medium-high heat. Sauté beef, onion and
celery for about 5 minutes, until beef is browned on all sides; drain.
Stir in remaining ingredients; bring to a boil. Reduce heat to low;
cover and simmer for 30 minutes, stirring occasionally, until beef
and noodles are tender. Makes 6 to 8 servings.

If you want to feel rich, just count all of the things
you have that money can't buy.
– Unknown

Hearty Chicken Soup

JoAnn

On weekends when there's more free time, I love to make soup from scratch with a freshly simmered chicken. On busy weeknights, though, this recipe is a real time-saver.

4 c. chicken broth
15-1/2 oz. can diced tomatoes
1/2 c. celery, thinly sliced
1/2 c. carrots, peeled and thinly
    sliced
1/2 c. onion, thinly sliced
2 T. white wine vinegar

1 t. soy sauce
1/4 t. dried basil
1/8 t. dried thyme
1/2 t. salt
1/4 t. pepper
1 deli roast chicken, diced or
    shredded

In a soup pot, combine all ingredients except chicken. Bring to a boil over medium-high heat. Reduce heat and simmer about 5 minutes. Add chicken; simmer an additional 15 minutes. Makes 6 servings.

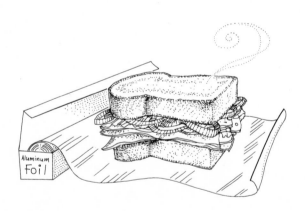

If family members will be dining at different times, fix sandwiches ahead of time, wrap in aluminum foil and refrigerate. Pop them into a toaster oven or under a broiler to heat...fresh, tasty and ready when you are!

Make-A-Meal
Sides

Creamed New Potatoes & Peas

Amy Hunt
Traphill, NC

This is one of my all-time favorite dishes...so good with a pan of cornbread! It's delicious made with new potatoes fresh from the garden, but if you're in a hurry you can use canned whole potatoes.

1 lb. new potatoes, peeled
2 T. butter
4 t. all-purpose flour

1 c. milk
15-oz. can peas, drained
salt and pepper to taste

Cut larger potatoes into chunks; cover potatoes with water in a saucepan. Over medium-high heat, cook until tender, about 15 to 20 minutes. Drain potatoes and set aside. In same saucepan over medium-low heat, melt butter. Stir in flour until smooth; blend in milk. Cook until thickened, stirring constantly. Add potatoes and peas. Stir to coat; heat through without boiling. Season to taste with salt and pepper. Serves 4.

Mix up a zingy oil & vinegar dressing to drizzle over crisp greens. Whisk together 3 tablespoons olive oil, 2 tablespoons white wine vinegar, 1/2 teaspoon minced garlic, 1/2 teaspoon Dijon mustard and 1/3 cup grated Parmesan cheese. Fresh!

Make-A-Meal Sides

Golden Parmesan Potatoes

Sue Klapper
Muskego, WI

*My husband and I just love roasted potatoes! This recipe is
so easy to prepare. The potatoes turn out very flavorful
thanks to the Parmesan cheese.*

2 15-oz. cans whole white
   potatoes, drained
1/4 c. butter, melted

3 T. grated Parmesan cheese
1 T. fresh parsley, minced
1/2 t. seasoned salt

Place potatoes in an ungreased 8"x8" baking pan. Drizzle butter over
potatoes; sprinkle with remaining ingredients. Bake, uncovered, at
350 degrees for 25 minutes, or until lightly golden. Makes 4 servings.

No built-in pantry in your kitchen? No problem! Pick up a
vintage kitchen hutch or china cabinet at a tag sale or flea market.
Freshen it up with a coat or two of paint in country colors.

Chive Mashed Potatoes

Jennie Gist
Gooseberry Patch

These buttery mashed potatoes are scrumptious...quick too! The potatoes don't need to be peeled, and the chives can be snipped right into the pan with kitchen shears.

2 lbs. redskin potatoes,
   quartered
1/2 c. butter
3 cloves garlic, chopped

3/4 c. fresh chives, snipped
Optional: 2 to 4 T. milk
salt and pepper to taste

In a large saucepan over medium-high heat, cover potatoes with water. Cook until tender, about 15 to 20 minutes. Drain potatoes; set aside. In same saucepan over medium heat, melt butter. Add garlic and cook briefly, until golden. Return potatoes to saucepan; add chives. Mash potatoes to desired consistency, adding a little milk if desired. Add salt and pepper to taste. Serves 6.

When you're shopping, let the kids pick out a new-to-them vegetable and help prepare it. Even picky eaters may be willing to try their very own veggie!

Cheesy Mashed Potato Pancakes

Anne Ptacnik
Yuma, CO

A tasty way to use up leftover mashed potatoes. Fry them in a heavy cast-iron skillet to create crispy, cheesy edges that everyone will love!

3 c. mashed potatoes	salt and pepper to taste
3/4 c. shredded Cheddar cheese	1/4 c. butter, divided

In a bowl, combine all ingredients except butter. Form into pancake-like patties, using 1/3 to 1/2 cup potato mixture for each. In a skillet over medium heat, melt 1/2 to one tablespoon butter. Add several patties to skillet. Cook until crisp and golden; turn to cook other side. Add more butter to skillet for each batch. Serve warm. Makes 6 to 8 servings.

Keep a tube or two of refrigerated crescent rolls on hand for quick-fix meals! Top dough with tomato sauce and cheese for a speedy pizza, use it to cover a chicken pot pie or even sprinkle with cinnamon-sugar and bake for a sweet treat to enjoy with an after-dinner coffee.

Stovetop Baked Beans

Bob Poerio
Munster, IN

A simple way to give canned pork & beans a little pizazz.

3 15-oz. cans pork & beans
1 to 2 T. brown sugar, packed
2 T. barbecue sauce

1 T. mustard
1/4 lb. bacon, chopped

Mix all ingredients except bacon in a saucepan. Simmer over medium heat. Meanwhile, in a skillet over medium-high heat, cook bacon until crisp. Drain bacon and stir into bean mixture. Continue to simmer over low heat for 15 minutes, stirring occasionally. Makes about 6 servings.

Are the kids having friends over for dinner? Bright-colored plastic flying disks make great no-spill holders for flimsy paper plates. Afterwards, everyone can take them home as keepsakes

Quick-Mix Poppy Seed Slaw

Lee Ann Paden
Visalia, CA

I wanted some coleslaw I could whip up fast, so I came up with this recipe myself. Now I make it all the time for family meals and potlucks. Mix it up first so it can chill while you prepare dinner.

16-oz. pkg. coleslaw mix
1/2 c. crushed pineapple, drained

1/2 c. red onion, diced
1/2 to 3/4 c. poppy seed salad dressing, divided

In a large bowl, combine coleslaw mix, pineapple and onion. Slowly add 1/2 cup salad dressing; toss to mix well. If not completely coated, add a little more dressing. Cover and chill for 30 minutes to one hour to allow flavors to blend. Serves 4 to 6.

Herb Biscuit Knots

Gladys Kielar
Perrysburg, OH

Fantastic and easy!

12-oz. tube refrigerated buttermilk biscuits
1/4 c. canola oil

1/2 t. garlic powder
1/2 t. Italian seasoning
1/8 t. salt

Cut each biscuit in half. Roll each piece into a 6-inch rope and tie in a loose knot. Place biscuits on a greased baking sheet. Bake at 400 degrees for about 9 to 11 minutes, until golden. Combine remaining ingredients in a small bowl. Immediately brush oil mixture over warm biscuits; brush again. Serve warm. Makes 20.

Anna Rae's Baby Limas

Juanita Proffitt
Pickens, SC

This is for everyone who likes a little spice in their lima beans! Anna Rae is my granddaughter who loves good ol' southern cooking. She also loves any kind of vegetable, which is odd for a five-year-old!

1 c. water
1 cube chicken bouillon
16-oz. pkg. frozen baby lima
   beans
1 slice bacon, chopped

1 clove garlic, lightly pressed
1/8 to 1/4 t. red pepper flakes
1/4 c. butter, softened
salt and pepper to taste

In a saucepan over medium heat, bring water and bouillon cube to a boil; stir. Add beans, bacon, garlic and red pepper flakes. Cover and turn heat to low. Cook about 25 minutes, until beans are tender. Drain; stir in butter, salt and pepper. Makes 5 to 6 servings.

Fresh vegetables are delicious and nutritious, but only if they're used promptly, so don't hesitate to use frozen vegetables instead. Flash-frozen soon after being harvested, frozen veggies retain nutrients and are a real time-saver too. Microwave them quickly or add them, still frozen, to a simmering pot of soup or a boiling pasta pot.

Lynda's Skillet Corn

Lynda Zickefoose
Lubbock, TX

I've had this simple recipe for so long that I don't remember where it came from. It's been enjoyed by my family for many years.

16-oz. pkg. frozen corn	1 t. salt
1/2 c. water	1/2 t. pepper
1/2 c. margarine	1/4 c. milk
1 T. sugar	1 T. all-purpose flour

In a skillet over medium heat, combine all ingredients except milk and flour. Cover and simmer for 15 to 20 minutes, stirring occasionally. In a small bowl, combine milk and flour; blend until smooth. Add milk mixture to skillet. Cook an additional 5 minutes over low heat, stirring constantly, until thickened. Serves 6.

Keep the cutting board from slipping while you chop! Set it on a piece of non-slip mesh easily found at home improvement stores... it's the same kind of pad used to keep area rugs from slipping.

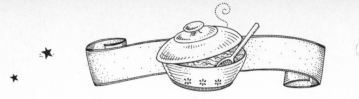

Grandma's Armenian Rice Pilaf

Betty Barsoian
Leominster, MA

This was a delicious favorite my grandmother used to make, then my mother took over the tradition. Now I make it for my own family. Be sure to use the smaller cans of condensed chicken broth.

2 10-1/2 oz. cans chicken broth
1/2 c. butter
1 c. vermicelli pasta, uncooked
   and broken into small pieces

2 c. long-cooking rice, uncooked
salt to taste

Bring broth to a boil in a saucepan or microwave-safe dish; remove from heat and set aside. In a skillet over medium heat, melt butter. Add uncooked vermicelli and cook until golden, stirring constantly. Add uncooked rice; continue cooking and stirring for several minutes, until golden. Add boiling broth and salt to vermicelli mixture. Reduce heat to low. Cover and cook for 20 minutes, until rice is tender and water is absorbed. Remove from heat; cover and let stand for 20 minutes before serving. Fluff with a fork and serve hot. Serves 8 to 10.

Fresh fruit makes a quick and colorful garnish for dinner plates. Try sliced oranges, kiwi or strawberries for a burst of color that's tasty too.

Garlic Butter Asparagus

Jennifer Jones
Fort Gordon, GA

*My sweet husband Travis makes this dish for us all the time. It's
especially terrific with baked salmon and rice.*

2 to 3 T. butter
2 to 3 cloves garlic, minced
1 lb. asparagus, trimmed

olive oil to taste
salt and pepper to taste

Melt butter in a skillet over medium heat. Add garlic and asparagus.
Cook for about 10 minutes, until crisp-tender. Just before removing
asparagus from skillet, drizzle with olive oil. Drain asparagus on paper
towels, if desired. Add salt and pepper to taste. Serves 4.

For speedy meal prep, place a bowl (or even a plastic grocery bag)
on your kitchen counter to collect scraps and trimmings
while you cook. Then just make one trip to the trash can
or compost bin when you're all done. Clever!

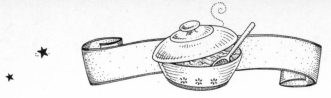

Roasted Garlic French Fries

*Ruth Cooksey
Plainfield, IN*

Feeding a crowd? It's so easy to double or triple this recipe.

16-oz. pkg. frozen French fries
2 T. garlic, minced
2 T. olive oil

2 T. fresh parsley, chopped
salt to taste

Bake French fries according to package instructions. In a small saucepan over medium heat, sauté garlic in olive oil just until garlic is golden. Drizzle oil mixture over baked French fries and toss to coat. Sprinkle with parsley and salt to taste. Makes 4 to 6 servings.

Parsley Baked Tomatoes

*Lydia Reaume
Ontario, Canada*

Quick, simple and yummy...a pleasing garnish for grilled steak.

4 tomatoes, halved
olive oil to taste
salt and pepper

1 T. fresh parsley, chopped
1 clove garlic, minced

Place tomatoes cut-side up in an ungreased 9"x9" baking pan; drizzle with olive oil. Season with salt and pepper. Mix parsley and garlic; sprinkle over tomatoes. Bake, uncovered, at 400 degrees for about 20 minutes, until tomatoes are hot and tender. Serves 4.

Create a table runner...a quick way to make any dinner more festive. Purchase cotton fabric in a cheerful seasonal or vintage print, hem or pink the edges and you're done!

Spicy Baked Chili Fries

Jo Blair
Afton, WY

My husband loves these French fries and always requests them. Serve them fresh and hot from the oven...make sure you have plenty of napkins!

1 t. chili powder
1 t. onion powder
1 t. garlic powder
1 t. seasoned salt
3 T. olive oil

3 baking potatoes, cut into wedges
Garnish: catsup or ranch salad dressing

Mix spices in a large container with a tight-fitting lid. Add oil and stir; add potato wedges. Put lid on container and seal tightly; shake vigorously to coat potatoes well. Arrange potatoes on an aluminum foil-lined baking sheet. Bake at 400 degrees for 15 minutes. Turn potatoes over and bake another 15 minutes, until tender and golden. Serve with Fry Sauce, catsup or ranch dressing for dipping. Makes 4 to 6 servings.

Fry Sauce:

1/2 c. catsup

1/2 c. mayonnaise

Stir catsup and mayonnaise together in a bowl.

A simple crockery bowl filled to the brim with ripe pears, apples and other fresh fruit makes an oh-so-simple centerpiece...it's a great way to encourage healthy snacking too.

Herbed Ripe Tomatoes

Sonia Daily
Rochester, MI

An easy recipe that's wonderful with juicy homegrown or farmers' market tomatoes. Perfect for a backyard barbecue side dish.

8 tomatoes, sliced
1/4 c. fresh parsley or cilantro, chopped
2 T. cider vinegar or tarragon vinegar

1/4 c. olive oil
2 T. mustard
1 clove garlic, crushed
1 t. salt
1/4 t. pepper

Place tomatoes in a shallow serving dish; set aside. Combine remaining ingredients in a covered jar. Add lid and shake well to mix. Pour mixture over tomatoes. Cover lightly; let stand at room temperature at least 20 minutes before serving. Makes 10 to 12 servings.

It's easy to save leftover fresh herbs for later use. Spoon chopped herbs into an ice cube tray, one tablespoon per cube. Cover with water and freeze. Frozen cubes can be dropped right into hot soups or stews.

Parmesan Supper Bread

Sharon Crider
Junction City, KS

With this recipe, it's oh-so easy to serve
freshly baked bread at dinnertime.

1-1/2 c. buttermilk baking mix
1 T. sugar
1 T. dried, minced onion
1/2 t. dried oregano

1 egg, beaten
1/4 c. milk
1/4 c. white wine or water
1/4 c. grated Parmesan cheese

In a bowl, combine all ingredients except cheese. Mix with a fork until soft dough forms. Spread in a greased 8" round cake pan; sprinkle with cheese. Bake at 400 degrees for 20 to 25 minutes, until golden. Cut into wedges and serve warm. Makes 6 to 8 servings.

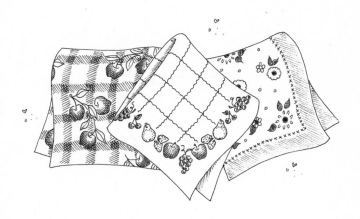

Add a little extra cheer to your kitchen! Turn vintage-style
tea towels into café curtains in a jiffy...simply attach
clip-on curtain rings.

Grandaddy's Skillet Cornbread

Jennifer Austin
Heath Springs, SC

This recipe was handed down from my grandaddy to my mother and now to me. This is the easiest and best-tasting cornbread. It's crispy and buttery on the outside...soft and moist inside. We eat it year 'round with soup. It's great for making cornbread dressing too.

2 c. self-rising cornmeal mix
2 T. butter, melted and cooled
   slightly
2 c. buttermilk

2 eggs, beaten
2 T. mayonnaise
1 T. shortening

In a bowl, combine all ingredients except shortening. Stir until creamy. Grease a cast-iron skillet well with shortening. Pour batter into skillet. Bake at 425 degrees for 15 minutes, or until a toothpick inserted in the center tests clean. Cut into wedges; serve warm. Makes 8 servings.

Make a scrapbook of Mom's favorite recipes...just going through the recipe box together will stir up sweet memories. Once favorite recipes are chosen, make copies and add family photos. Taken to the nearest copy shop, duplicates can quickly and easily be made to share with family & friends.

Spicy Black Beans & Rice

Aubrey Nygren-Earl
Taylorsville, UT

This flavorful dish goes well with just about any
Mexican meal...it's always a hit!

1 t. olive oil
1 onion, chopped
2 cloves garlic, minced
3/4 c. long-cooking rice,
    uncooked
1-1/2 c. low-sodium chicken
    broth

1 t. ground cumin
1/4 t. cayenne pepper
1/4 t. garlic powder
1/8 t. paprika
15-1/2 oz. can black beans,
    drained
15-1/2 oz. can diced tomatoes

Heat oil in a stockpot over medium-high heat. Add onion and garlic;
sauté for 4 minutes. Add uncooked rice; sauté for 2 minutes. Stir in
broth and seasonings. Bring to a boil; reduce heat to low. Cover and
cook for 20 minutes. Stir in beans and undrained tomatoes. Cook for
another 5 to 10 minutes, until heated through. Makes 8 servings.

Looking for a tasty change from rice and potatoes? Try polenta
in ready-to-use tubes, found near the sausage section in the
supermarket. Slice it 1/2-inch thick and pan-fry in olive oil until
golden. Top with warmed spaghetti sauce or Mexican-style
seasoned beans...yum!

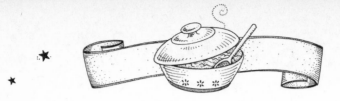

Honey-Roasted Carrots

Jill Ball
Highland, UT

Kids especially like carrots fixed this simple way.

3 lbs. carrots, peeled and
    quartered lengthwise
1 T. olive oil

1/2 t. salt
1/4 t. pepper
2 T. honey

In a large bowl, toss together carrots, oil, salt and pepper. Spread on a 15"x10" jelly-roll pan. Bake, uncovered, at 400 degrees for 30 minutes, or until carrots are tender. Place under broiler for 2 to 4 minutes, until golden. Toss with honey; serve warm. Makes 8 servings.

Golden Roasted Cauliflower

Sandy Glennen
Dandridge, TN

The only way my husband likes cooked cauliflower...he loves this!

1 head cauliflower, cut into
    bite-size flowerets

2 T. olive oil
1/4 t. salt

Toss cauliflower with oil and salt in a large bowl. Spread in a single layer in a 15"x10" jelly-roll pan. Bake, uncovered, at 450 degrees for 25 to 35 minutes, stirring and turning occasionally, until tender and golden. Serves 4 to 6.

A generous square of checked homespun or flowered calico makes a cozy liner for a basket of warm rolls or muffins.

Make-A-Meal *Sides*

Buttermilk Biscuits

Sharon Moase
Prince Edward Island, Canada

At our house, every Friday was baking day. Mom always told me the secret to tender biscuits was to use buttermilk. One day I made the biscuits with 2% milk and they turned out like hockey pucks... lesson learned!

3 c. all-purpose flour
2 T. baking powder
1/2 t. salt

1/2 c. shortening
2 eggs, lightly beaten
1 c. buttermilk

Mix flour, baking powder and salt in a large bowl. Add shortening; use a pastry cutter to blend together. Add eggs and buttermilk; stir until moistened. On a floured pastry board, pat out dough to desired thickness. Cut out biscuits with a biscuit cutter; place on a baking sheet sprayed with non-stick vegetable spray. Bake at 400 degrees until lightly golden, about 15 minutes. Makes about 15.

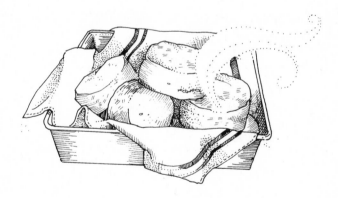

The secret to tender steamed rice: cook long-cooking rice as the package directs. When it's done, uncover the pan, top with a folded tea towel and put the lid back on. Let stand for 5 to 10 minutes before serving. The towel will absorb any excess moisture.

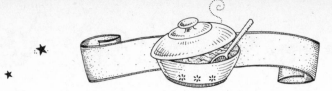

Best-Ever Fried Potatoes

Kristin Pittis
Dennison, OH

A terrific comfort food dish for breakfast, lunch or dinner.

2 T. butter
2 T. oil
5 to 6 potatoes, peeled and cut
    into 1/2-inch cubes
1 onion, diced

1 green or red pepper, diced
1/2 t. smoked paprika
3/4 t. salt
1/4 t. pepper

In a large non-stick skillet over medium-high heat, melt butter with oil. Add potatoes, onion and green or red pepper. Sprinkle with seasonings; stir to coat well. Reduce heat to medium. Cover and cook, stirring frequently, for 25 to 30 minutes, until potatoes are golden and tender. Serves 4 to 6.

For hearty salads in a snap, keep unopened cans and jars of diced
tomatoes, black olives, chickpeas and marinated artichokes
in the fridge. They'll be chilled and ready to toss with
fresh greens or cooked pasta at a moment's notice.

Make-A-Meal Sides

Savory Green Beans

Christina Mendoza
Alamogordo, NM

This is our favorite tried & true way to fix fresh green beans.
The tomatoes are a delicious touch!

5 slices bacon, quartered
1/4 c. onion, chopped
1/4 c. roma tomato, diced
2 T. butter

2 T. canola oil
1 lb. green beans, trimmed and
    cut into bite-size pieces

In a large skillet over medium-high heat, cook bacon until almost crisp. Add onion and tomato to skillet; cook and stir until light golden. Remove bacon and set aside; reserve drippings in skillet. Crumble or chop bacon; return to drippings in skillet. Add butter, oil and beans; cook and stir until tender, about 8 minutes. Makes 2 to 4 servings.

Start a family tradition...have a candlelight dinner once a week with your children. A table set with lit tapers, snowy-white napkins and the best china will let your kids know they are special. They'll be on their best behavior too!

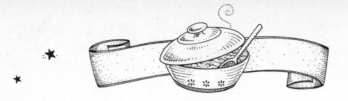

Sautéed Greens & Warm Pecan Dressing

Gloria Lopez
Austin, TX

Fresh from the garden...a delectable way to serve greens. Yum!

2 T. balsamic vinegar
1 T. mustard
2 t. honey
1/2 c. pecans, coarsely chopped

2 T. canola or olive oil
1 to 2 bunches kale, spinach or
    Swiss chard, chopped

In a small bowl, combine vinegar, mustard, honey and pecans; set aside. Heat oil in a large skillet over medium heat. Add greens and toss until well coated with oil. Cook and stir until greens are wilted but still bright green. Add vinegar mixture to skillet, stirring lightly. Cook for about one more minute and serve immediately. Serves 6.

Set little ones down with a bowl of fruit-flavored cereal rings
and a piece of dental floss...they can make cereal necklaces
(and nibble away!) while you're getting dinner ready.

Easy Almond Rice

Lillian Lane
Roseville, CA

A former neighbor shared this simple recipe with me
and it has become a family favorite.

3-1/2 c. boiling water
4 to 5 cubes beef bouillon
1/2 c. butter
2 c. long-cooking rice, uncooked

4 to 5 T. soy sauce
4 to 5 green onions, chopped
1/2 c. slivered almonds

Combine boiling water and bouillon cubes; stir until dissolved and set aside. Melt butter in a heavy skillet over medium heat. Add uncooked rice to skillet; cook and stir for one to 2 minutes. Add bouillon mixture to rice; reduce heat. Cover and simmer for 20 to 30 minutes, until water is absorbed. Add remaining ingredients; stir and heat through. Makes 8 to 10 servings.

Need a quick, safe cleaner for your stainless steel sink?
Baking soda cleans and shines almost effortlessly. Just grab
the box of baking soda from your pantry, apply directly
to the sink and wipe gently with a damp sponge.

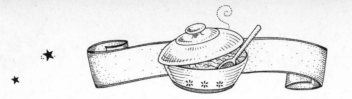

Quick Brown Bread

Eleanor Dionne
Beverly, MA

I've been making this bread for many years whenever the weather gets colder. If you like, use a cup of buttermilk instead of the milk and vinegar. This bread goes very well with homemade baked beans.

1 c. milk
1 T. white vinegar
2 c. whole-wheat flour
1 t. salt
1-1/2 t. baking powder

1/2 t. baking soda
1 egg, beaten
1/2 c. molasses
1/4 c. shortening, melted and
  cooled, or oil

Combine milk and vinegar in a small bowl; let stand for a few minutes. In a separate large bowl, combine flour, salt, baking powder and baking soda. Mix thoroughly and set aside. Add remaining ingredients to milk mixture. Add milk mixture to flour mixture; stir just enough to barely mix. Pour batter into a well-greased 9"x5" loaf pan. Bake at 350 degrees for about 30 minutes, until a toothpick inserted in the center tests clean. Makes one loaf.

Need a gift in a jiffy for a teacher, a neighbor or a friend with a new baby? Give a loaf of freshly baked quick bread wrapped in a pretty tea towel...it's sure to be appreciated.

Quick Squash Sauté

JoAnn

My whole family likes this quick-to-fix side. It's especially tasty with squash from the farmers' market, but we enjoy it year 'round with squash from the supermarket's produce section.

2 T. olive oil
1 onion, sliced
4 zucchini and/or yellow
   squash, halved lengthwise
   and sliced

1 t. dried oregano
1 t. garlic powder
salt and pepper to taste

Heat olive oil in a large skillet over medium-high heat. Add onion; sauté for about one minute. Add remaining ingredients. Continue cooking over medium heat until vegetables are crisp-tender, about 10 minutes. Makes 4 to 6 servings.

Make a big pot of vegetable soup using vegetables left over from dinner. Keep a container in the freezer just for saving leftover veggies. When you have enough, thaw and place in a slow cooker. Add a can of tomato sauce, water to cover and favorite seasonings to taste. Cover and cook on low all day...delicious and economical!

Oven-Baked Mexican Rice

Estelle Weddle
Salt Lake City, UT

My family loves Mexican food. Whenever we went out to eat, everyone always exclaimed over the delicious rice. A friend gave me a traditional rice recipe, but it came out too sticky. So I put my spin on an oven version...now the rice comes out perfectly every time! It's an excellent side dish for tacos, enchiladas and many more Mexican dishes. Enjoy!

2 T. butter or olive oil
1 onion, chopped
1-1/2 c. long-cooking rice,
   uncooked

1 t. garlic, minced
2 c. chicken broth
1-1/4 c. tomato juice

Heat butter or oil in a skillet over medium heat. Add onion; cook until translucent. Add rice and garlic. Cook and stir until rice is lightly golden. Stir in remaining ingredients; bring to a boil. Transfer mixture to a greased 2-quart casserole dish. Cover and bake at 350 degrees for 25 minutes, or until rice is tender. Makes 4 to 6 servings.

Keep a few packages of frozen ravioli, tortellini and pierogies tucked in the freezer for easy meal-making anytime. Quickly cooked and topped with your favorite jar sauce, they're terrific as either a side dish or a meatless main.

Cheese & Garlic Biscuits

Lori Vincent
Alpine, UT

*This is my family's favorite bread to enjoy with
a steamy bowl of soup!*

2 c. biscuit baking mix
2/3 c. milk
1/2 c. shredded Cheddar cheese

1/4 c. butter, melted
1/4 t. garlic powder

In a bowl, combine biscuit mix, milk and cheese. Stir until soft dough
forms; beat vigorously for 30 seconds. Drop dough by tablespoonfuls
onto a parchment paper-lined or greased baking sheet. Bake at
450 degrees for 8 to 10 minutes, until lightly golden. Mix melted
butter and garlic powder; brush over warm biscuits. Serve warm.
Makes 1-1/2 dozen.

For a festive, healthy dessert in a jiffy, layer fresh berries
with creamy vanilla yogurt in stemmed glasses.

Chopped Salad

Arlene Smulski
Lyons, IL

This salad is fast and easy! Add a cup of cubed cooked chicken to turn it into a hearty main-dish salad.

4 c. romaine lettuce, torn
1 c. broccoli, chopped
1/2 c. carrots, peeled and chopped
1/2 c. ranch salad dressing

1/2 c. shredded sharp Cheddar cheese
4 slices bacon, crisply cooked and crumbled

In a large salad bowl, combine lettuce, broccoli, carrots and salad dressing; toss well. Top with cheese and bacon; serve immediately. Makes 4 servings.

Turn any simple salad into a pretty layered salad. Just add favorite salad ingredients, one layer at a time, into a glass serving bowl. Toss with dressing just before serving.

Make-A-Meal Sides

Chilled Broccoli Salad

Colleen Hale
La Vernia, TX

Years ago, this was the only way my kids would eat broccoli!

1 large or 2 small bunches
   broccoli
8-oz. bottle Italian salad
   dressing

Garnish: grated Parmesan
   cheese

Rinse broccoli; drain. Trim broccoli and cut into separate stalks, leaving stalks long. Arrange broccoli in a microwave-safe dish. Do not add any extra water. Cover with plastic wrap; vent. Microwave on high for about 7 minutes. Drain any liquid from dish. Drizzle broccoli with salad dressing; sprinkle with cheese. Cover with fresh plastic wrap; chill until serving time. Makes 4 to 6 servings.

Keep vegetables fresh and nutritious! Wrap them in paper towels and refrigerate in unsealed plastic bags in the crisper drawer. Don't rinse veggies until you're ready to cook them.

Kickin' Coleslaw

Peggy Market
Elida, OH

This zesty coleslaw adds pizazz to any meal...it always accompanies our barbecues. It tastes even better the next day, if it lasts that long! Mix it up in the morning or the night before so it can chill.

16-oz. pkg. coleslaw mix
1/2 c. creamy horseradish sauce
1 T. prepared horseradish
1 c. mayonnaise

1/4 c. sugar
2 T. vinegar
1/4 t. salt
1/4 t. pepper

Place coleslaw mix in a large salad bowl. In a separate bowl, combine remaining ingredients. Blend well; pour over coleslaw mix. Cover and refrigerate at least 3 hours before serving. Serves 8.

Mom's Mayonnaise Muffins

Polly McCallum
Palatka, FL

I loved it when my mom made these muffins. They were one of the first things I learned to bake too!

2 c. self-rising flour
1/2 c. mayonnaise

1 c. milk
1 T. sugar

In a bowl, combine all ingredients. Mix well and spoon into greased muffin cups, filling 2/3 full. Bake at 400 degrees for about 12 minutes, until golden. Makes one dozen.

Music sets the tone for pleasant family dinnertimes. Choose favorites together or listen to something different...just keep the music low so table talk can continue.

Rainbow Pasta Salad

LaShelle Brown
Mulvane, KS

This is my husband's all-time favorite pasta salad. He requests it at all of our summer events. Add cubes of ham or salami for an even heartier salad.

4 c. rainbow rotini pasta, uncooked
1 cucumber, quartered lengthwise and sliced
1 tomato, chopped

4-oz. can sliced black olives, drained
1 c. ranch salad dressing
1/3 c. Italian salad dressing

Cook pasta according to package directions; drain and rinse with cold water. In a large salad bowl, combine pasta, cucumber, tomato and olives; mix well. In a separate bowl, mix salad dressings together. Add to pasta mixture; toss to coat. Cover and refrigerate for at least one hour. Serves 8.

Make-ahead sides are super time-savers for busy-day meals. Assemble in the morning or the night before, cover and refrigerate, then just pop in the oven and serve. Make-ahead salads are even speedier...they can go straight from the fridge to the dinner table!

Quick & Easy Italian Slaw

April Garner
Independence, KY

*This recipe is great to make in the morning so it's ready for supper.
I like to use a yellow pepper in the summertime and a red pepper
for fall...it looks so pretty!*

16-oz. pkg. coleslaw mix
1 red or yellow pepper, chopped
light brown sugar to taste

8-oz. bottle zesty Italian salad
dressing

In a salad bowl, combine coleslaw mix and pepper. Sprinkle lightly
with brown sugar; drizzle with salad dressing and toss well. Cover
and refrigerate for at least 30 minutes to allow flavors to blend.
Serves 8.

To keep salad fixin's in a crisper that's extra clean, wash the
crisper drawers with one part bleach to 4 parts water.
Rinse and dry well.

Best-Ever Garlic Bread

Vickie

A warm loaf of this irresistible garlic bread turns plain ol' spaghetti & meatballs into a feast! To save time, whip up the butter spread ahead of time and keep it in the fridge for up to two days.

3/4 c. butter, softened
6 T. mayonnaise
3/4 c. grated Parmesan cheese
2 T. fresh parsley, chopped

3 cloves garlic, minced
1/2 t. dried oregano
1 loaf French bread, halved
   lengthwise

In a small bowl, blend together all ingredients except bread. Spread butter mixture over cut sides of bread. Wrap bread in 2 pieces of aluminum foil; place cut-side up on a baking sheet. Bake at 375 degrees for 20 minutes. Unwrap bread and discard foil; place bread on a broiler pan. Broil until golden, about 2 minutes. Slice; serve warm. Makes one loaf.

The most indispensable ingredient of all good home cooking: love for those you are cooking for.

– Sophia Loren

Crunchy Potato Wedges

Beth Bundy
Long Prairie, MN

*A special recipe from one of my grandma's very old
cookbooks...it's a keeper!*

1 egg white, beaten
1/2 t. salt
1/4 t. pepper

1/2 c. corn flake cereal, crushed
2 lbs. baking potatoes, peeled
and cut into thin wedges

In a shallow bowl, whisk together egg white, salt and pepper. Place cereal crumbs in a separate shallow bowl. Dip each potato wedge into egg mixture and then roll in crumbs. Place wedges on a well-greased baking sheet. Bake at 450 degrees for 25 minutes, until tender and golden. Serves 4 to 6.

Looking for something to keep the kids busy while you're making dinner? Just cover a table with plain white freezer paper and add plenty of crayons...they can create a tablecloth masterpiece!

Lori's Quick Potato Salad

Lori Simmons
Princeville, IL

If you want a quick and tasty cool side dish, this is it! I make a double batch for potlucks. Garnish with deviled eggs and sweet pickles, if you like.

1 lb. potatoes, peeled and
    quartered
1/4 c. mayonnaise

1 t. mustard
1/2 t. dried, minced onion
1/4 t. salt

In a large saucepan, cover potatoes with water. Bring to a boil over medium-high heat. Cook until potatoes are tender, 15 to 20 minutes. Drain; place in a bowl and allow to cool. Stir in remaining ingredients. Cover and chill before serving. Makes 4 to 6 servings.

For a fun after-school snack that's ready in a jiffy, stuff a hollowed-out apple with peanut butter and raisins.

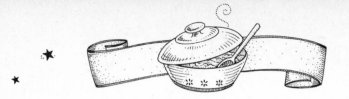

Classic Waldorf Salad

Cheryl Panning
Wabash, IN

I started making this tried & true salad when I was a new bride.
Forty years later, my husband still requests it!

2 c. Red Delicious apples, cored
   and diced
1 c. celery, sliced
1/2 c. broken pecans or walnuts
1/4 c. mayonnaise

1 c. frozen whipped topping,
   thawed
1 T. sugar
1/2 t. lemon juice
1/8 t. salt

In a serving bowl, combine apples, celery and nuts. In a separate
bowl, blend remaining ingredients; fold into apple mixture. Cover and
chill until serving time. Serves 4 to 6.

An easy way to core apples and pears! Just slice fruit
in half and then use a melon baller to scoop out
the center, core and all.

Speedy Potluck
& Party Foods

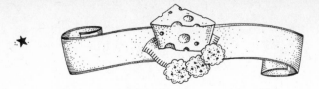

Crowd-Pleaser Taco Salad

Marla Caldwell
Forest, IN

This dish is always requested at our school sports banquets...the kids love it! We parents consider ourselves lucky if there's any left by the time we go through the food line.

2 lbs. ground beef
1 onion, chopped
2/3 c. water
2 1-1/4 oz. pkgs. taco
   seasoning mix, divided
2 heads iceberg lettuce, chopped
4 tomatoes, chopped

1-1/2 c. sliced black olives,
   drained
2 c. shredded Cheddar cheese
8-oz. bottle Catalina salad
   dressing
16-oz. pkg. nacho cheese tortilla
   chips, crushed

In a large skillet over medium heat, brown beef with onion; drain. Stir in water and one package of taco seasoning; simmer for 5 minutes. Remove from heat; allow to cool completely. In a large serving bowl, mix together lettuce, tomatoes, olives, cheese and remaining package of taco seasoning. Add beef mixture; toss together to combine. Just before serving, toss with salad dressing; top with the crushed chips. Makes 20 servings.

Turn your budding chefs loose in the kitchen! Get a group of kids together to whip up a quick & easy meal like Crowd-Pleaser Taco Salad. Not only is it a great way to teach kids some cooking basics, they'll have a ball cooking with friends.

Mouthwatering Chicken Quesadillas

Raegan Casto
Charleston, WV

This is my husband's absolute favorite dish. The ladies at work don't mind leftovers when I bring this! It's a huge crowd-pleaser and a favorite of just about everyone I know.

2 to 3 T. oil
6 to 8 boneless, skinless
   chicken breasts, cut into
   bite-size pieces
1 onion, diced
1 to 2 green peppers, diced
seasoning salt and pepper
   to taste

1-1/3 c. water
2 1-1/4 oz. pkgs. taco
   seasoning mix
10 10-inch flour tortillas
2 to 3 c. shredded Cheddar
   cheese

In a large skillet, heat oil over medium heat. Sauté chicken, onion, green peppers, salt and pepper until chicken is cooked through; drain. Add water and both packages of taco seasoning; simmer for 5 minutes. Lightly coat 2 baking sheets with non-stick vegetable spray. Lay tortillas flat on baking sheets. On half of tortilla, add a sprinkle of cheese, some of chicken mixture and another sprinkle of cheese. Fold tortilla in half and slide to end of baking sheet. Continue filling tortillas until baking sheets are full, slightly overlapping to help hold in the stuffing. Bake at 350 degrees for 10 to 15 minutes, until heated through and edges are golden. Serves 6 to 8.

Watch yard sales for a vintage salad dressing server...it's just as handy for serving up salsa, guacamole and sour cream for Tex-Mex dishes!

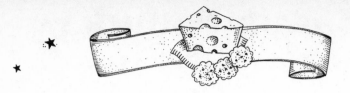

Italian Hamburger Mac

Ben Gothard
Jemison, AL

When I was a kid, my mom always made a dish like this...I could just eat the entire pot full. Now that I'm grown, I have put my own spin on the dish. This one's for you, Mama!

2 lbs. ground beef chuck
1 onion, diced
salt and pepper to taste
3 c. elbow macaroni, uncooked
2 46-oz. cans tomato juice

1 T. dried oregano
2 t. dried basil
1 t. garlic salt
1 t. onion salt

In a skillet over medium heat, cook beef until browned. Add onion, salt and pepper. Continue cooking for 5 minutes; drain. Transfer beef mixture to a stockpot; add uncooked macaroni and remaining ingredients. Bring to a boil over medium-high heat. Reduce heat; cover and simmer for about 20 minutes, stirring frequently, just until macaroni is tender. Remove from stove. Let cool for 10 minutes before serving to allow mixture to thicken. Makes 8 to 10 servings.

Festive trimmings can turn even a plain meal into a feast. Pick up some inexpensive, brightly colored napkins and table coverings at the nearest dollar store and you're already halfway to a party!

Beefy Shellaroni

Peggy Market
Elida, OH

This is a much-requested dish for our church potlucks...it always disappears very quickly! Serve with warm garlic bread and a tasty salad for a satisfying meal.

16-oz. pkg. medium macaroni
   shells, uncooked
2 lbs. ground beef

1 c. catsup
1 t. chili powder
salt and pepper to taste

Cook macaroni in a stockpot according to package instructions; drain. Rinse macaroni in a colander and return to stockpot. Meanwhile, in a large skillet over medium heat, brown beef; drain. Add beef and remaining ingredients to cooked macaroni in stockpot; mix well. Cover and simmer over low heat for 15 minutes, stirring occasionally. Serves 8 to 10.

At sit-down dinners, encourage table talk among guests who don't know each other well...just write each person's name on both sides of his or her placecard so other guests can see it!

Freezer Meatballs

Gretchen Brown
Forest Grove, OR

I love to be able to just pull meatballs out of the freezer on a busy evening and add to some spaghetti sauce. My family loves this meal and it is so quick & easy.

4 eggs
2 c. dry bread crumbs
2 T. dried, minced onion

2 t. Worcestershire sauce
1/2 t. pepper
4 lbs. lean ground beef

Beat eggs in a large bowl; stir in remaining ingredients except beef. Add beef; mix well and form into one-inch balls. Place meatballs in single layers in ungreased baking pans. Bake, uncovered, at 400 degrees for 10 to 15 minutes, or until no longer pink; drain. Cool; place meatballs into freezer bags or containers, about 30 meatballs each. May be frozen for up to 3 months. Makes about 12 dozen.

Serve sliders at your next party...everyone will love them! Mix up your favorite meatball or meatloaf recipe, then form the mixture into flattened mini burgers. Pan-fry, grill or bake as desired and serve on mini sandwich buns or dinner rolls.

Swedish Meatballs or Kottbuller

Carol Brinkman
Onarga, IL

In my family, it's just not Christmas without these meatballs being served! Last year my grandson ate 27 meatballs at our get-together and asked for more before his father stepped in and said, "Enough!" I may have to double the recipe if this keeps up!

2 slices bread, crusts removed
1 c. milk
2 eggs, lightly beaten
2 lbs. lean ground beef
1/2 lb. ground pork shoulder
2 T. onion, minced
1 t. sugar
2 to 3 t. salt
1/2 t. pepper
1/4 c. butter
2 T. all-purpose flour
1/2 to 1 c. milk

In a small bowl, soak bread slices in milk; add eggs. In a separate large bowl, pour bread mixture over beef and pork. Mix with your hands or a stand mixer on low speed until well blended. Add onion, sugar, salt and pepper; continue to mix until light and fluffy. Form into walnut-size balls. Melt butter in a large skillet over medium heat; add meatballs. Cover skillet and allow to steam over low heat for 20 to 25 minutes, until browned. Remove meatballs to a plate, reserving drippings in skillet; keep warm while making gravy. Over low heat, stir flour into drippings in skillet. Thin with milk to desired consistency; cook and stir until thickened. Serve meatballs with gravy. Makes about 12 dozen.

Making lots of meatballs? Grab a melon baller and start scooping...you'll be done in record time!

Stovetop Mexican Macaroni

Theresa Wehmeyer
Rosebud, MO

This hearty dish is welcome on any potluck table! It's easy to double for a larger group too.

16-oz. pkg. cavatappi pasta or elbow macaroni, uncooked
1 lb. ground beef
3/4 c. onion, chopped
15-oz. can petite diced tomatoes
10-3/4 oz. can tomato soup
8-oz. can tomato sauce
1-1/4 oz. pkg. taco seasoning mix
Garnish: shredded Mexican-blend cheese

Cook pasta or macaroni according to package directions; drain. Meanwhile, brown beef and onion in a Dutch oven over medium heat; drain. Add remaining ingredients except garnish to beef mixture; bring to a boil. Reduce heat to low. Simmer, uncovered, for 5 minutes, or until thickened. Stir in cooked pasta and heat through. Top servings with cheese. Serves 6.

Quickie Cornbread

Dawn Schlauderaff
Brooklyn Park, MN

A friend at work shared this two-ingredient wonder with me.

8-1/2 oz. pkg. cornbread mix   14-3/4 oz. can creamed corn

In a bowl, stir together cornbread mix and creamed corn until moistened. Pour into an 8"x8" baking pan sprayed with non-stick vegetable spray. Bake at 400 degrees for 20 to 25 minutes, until set and golden. Cut into squares. Makes 8 servings.

Be sure to have take-out containers on hand to send guests home with leftovers...if there are any!

Speedy Potluck & Party Foods

Mexican Pasta Bake

Jan Sherwood
Carpentersville, IL

We first enjoyed this dish at a football party as a side with grilled chicken and brats. Spice it up with medium or hot salsa.

3 c. rotini pasta, uncooked
2 16-oz. jars mild thick & chunky salsa
1 c. cottage cheese
16-oz. can black beans, drained and rinsed

16-oz. can corn, drained
2 c. shredded sharp Cheddar cheese, divided
1/4 c. fresh cilantro, chopped

Cook pasta as directed on package; drain. In a large bowl, mix cooked pasta, salsa, cottage cheese, beans, corn and one cup shredded cheese. Spoon into a deep 13"x9" baking pan sprayed with non-stick vegetable spray. Sprinkle remaining cheese on top. Bake, uncovered, at 375 degrees for 25 to 30 minutes, until hot and bubbly. Sprinkle with cilantro. Makes 10 to 12 servings.

A helpful tip for any potluck buffet table...stack the plates at the beginning, but save the flatware, napkins and beverages for the end of the line. So much easier to handle!

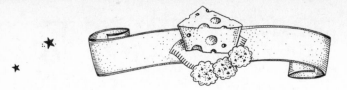

Cheesy Chicken & Angel Hair

Mary Little
Franklin, TN

This recipe was given to me by my sister-in-law and we've enjoyed it at many family gatherings. I use canned chicken to speed it up.

7-oz. pkg. angel hair pasta,
   uncooked
1 onion, chopped
1 green pepper, chopped
1/4 c. margarine
2 to 4 c. cooked chicken,
   chopped

3/4 lb. pasteurized process
   cheese spread, diced
16-oz. can green peas, drained
10-oz. can diced tomatoes with
   green chiles

Cook pasta as directed on package; drain. Meanwhile, in a small skillet over medium heat, sauté onion and green pepper in margarine. In a large bowl, combine onion mixture, cooked pasta and remaining ingredients. Mix thoroughly and transfer to a greased 3-quart casserole dish. Bake, uncovered, at 350 degrees for 30 minutes, or until heated through. Makes 8 to 10 servings.

Make-ahead casseroles are super time-savers for school potlucks or church carry-ins after work. Assemble the night before, cover and refrigerate, then just pop in the oven...soon you're on your way!

Speedy Potluck & Party Foods

Mom's "Chicken Wing" Casserole
Graceann Frederico
Bluffton, SC

Since chicken wings can be expensive, I created this budget-friendly casserole version. When I made this recipe for my church fellowship, it won the Grand Prize! It was great fun and I am happy to share it. For variety, omit the tortillas and top with crushed tortilla chips, or replace half of the Cheddar cheese with blue cheese.

4 8-inch flour tortillas
1 to 2 T. olive oil
8-oz. bottle hot pepper sauce or
    buffalo wing sauce, divided
4 boneless chicken breasts,
    cooked and shredded
1 c. light sour cream

2 8-oz. pkgs. low-fat cream
    cheese, softened
3 stalks celery, thinly sliced
1-oz. pkg. ranch dip mix
8-oz. pkg. shredded sharp
    Cheddar cheese, divided

Spritz tortillas with olive oil; place on a broiler pan. Broil for 2 to 3 minutes on each side, until tortillas begin to char a little and puff up. Remove and set aside. Spray a 13"x9" baking pan with non-stick vegetable spray. Spread some sauce lightly in bottom of pan. Line bottom of pan with 2 tortillas. Moisten with a little sauce; set aside. In a bowl, mix chicken, sour cream, cream cheese, celery, dip mix, remaining sauce and one cup shredded cheese. Mix until blended; pat half of mixture into pan. Add 2 more tortillas and moisten with sauce. Top with remaining chicken mixture and cheese. Bake, uncovered, at 350 degrees for 30 to 35 minutes, until bubbly and cheese is melted. Serves 6 to 8.

Instead of setting up one or two long dining tables, scatter several smaller ones around the room so friends can chat easily.

Ziti Bake Supreme

Kristin Freeman
Dundas, MN

Always a hit when friends come for dinner!

16-oz. pkg. ziti pasta, uncooked
32-oz. jar spaghetti sauce
16-oz. container ricotta cheese

1/4 c. grated Parmesan cheese
2 c. shredded mozzarella cheese,
  divided

Cook pasta according to package directions; drain and return to stockpot. Stir sauce into cooked pasta. Spoon half of pasta mixture into a greased 13"x9" baking pan. In a bowl, combine ricotta cheese, Parmesan cheese and one cup mozzarella cheese. Spread all of cheese mixture over pasta mixture. Add remaining pasta mixture; top with remaining mozzarella cheese. Bake, uncovered, at 350 degrees for 30 to 40 minutes, until hot and bubbly. Makes 8 to 10 servings.

Create a cozy Italian restaurant feel for your next pasta dinner.
Toss a red & white checked tablecloth over the table, light drip
candles in empty bottles and add a basket of warm garlic bread.

Speedy Potluck & Party Foods

Sausage & Rice Casserole

Liz Watanabe
Kent, WA

My mom has made this yummy casserole for several years. I always thought it must be very complicated because it was so delicious. One night we were having dinner at Mom & Dad's. My husband found out how good it is and I had no choice but to try making it myself! It's comfort food that's very easy to prepare, and yet scrumptious enough to serve to guests.

2 lbs. ground pork sausage
1 onion, chopped
3 to 4 c. celery, chopped
1/8 t. pepper, or to taste

9 c. water
2 c. long-cooking rice, uncooked
3 2-oz. envs. chicken noodle
   soup mix, uncooked

In a large, deep skillet over medium heat, cook sausage, onion and celery, stirring often to break up sausage. Drain, reserving 1-1/2 tablespoons drippings in skillet with sausage mixture. Add pepper and set aside. Meanwhile, in a very large stockpot over high heat, bring water to a boil. Add uncooked rice and soup mix to boiling water; stir well and add sausage mixture. Stir to mix completely; mixture will be very watery. Transfer to a greased deep 3-quart casserole dish. Bake, uncovered, at 350 degrees for 20 minutes. Remove from oven; stir. Cover and bake an additional 30 to 40 minutes, until liquid is absorbed and rice is tender. Makes 10 to 12 servings.

For an elegant yet quick last-minute appetizer, toss a drained jar of Italian antipasto mix with bite-size cubes of mozzarella cheese. Serve with cocktail picks. No one needs to know you stopped at the market on the way to the party!

Cheeseburger Casserole

Heather Johnson
Liberty, MO

Any time there's a gathering of family & friends that includes kids, this dish is a must! There's never any left, so clean-up is a snap too.

2 lbs. ground beef
1.35-oz. pkg. onion soup mix
10-3/4 oz. can cream of
  mushroom soup
10-3/4 oz. can Cheddar cheese
  soup

20-oz. pkg. frozen potato puffs
Garnish: mustard, catsup and
  other favorite toppings

Brown beef in a large skillet over medium heat; drain. Add soup mix; stir to coat all of the beef. Add soups and stir until blended. Transfer mixture to a lightly greased 13"x9" baking pan; arrange potato puffs on top. Bake, uncovered, at 350 degrees for 50 to 55 minutes, until golden. Garnish as desired. Makes 8 to 10 servings.

Everybody loves burgers...and they don't have to be ordinary!
Ground turkey, chicken, ground pork sausage and veggie burgers
are all scrumptious. Try the seasoning blends found at the meat
counter like Italian, Mexican, Southwest or Mediterranean...yum!

Sloppy Joe Bake

Diana Chaney
Olathe, KS

A terrific casserole version of a family favorite! It's simple to whip up a double batch for potlucks and parties too.

1-1/2 lbs. ground beef
1/4 c. onion, chopped
1/4 c. green pepper, chopped
15-1/2 oz. can Sloppy Joe sauce
8-oz. pkg. shredded Cheddar
   cheese

2 c. biscuit baking mix
2 eggs, beaten
1 c. milk

In a skillet over medium heat, brown beef, onion and green pepper; drain. Stir in sauce. Spoon mixture into a greased 13"x9" baking pan; sprinkle with cheese. In a bowl, stir together remaining ingredients just until blended. Spoon over cheese. Bake, uncovered, at 400 degrees for about 25 minutes, until golden. Cut into squares. Serves 8.

Luau Baked Beans

Susan Jacobs
Vista, CA

Great for picnics and cookouts! I served this easy dish at the luau we hosted for our daughter when she received her doctorate degree.

1 lb. bacon, cut into 1-inch
   pieces
1/2 onion, chopped
16-oz. bottle barbecue sauce

2 28-oz. cans baked beans,
   drained
20-oz. can crushed pineapple,
   drained

In a large skillet over medium heat, cook bacon to desired crispness; drain. Add onion; cook with bacon until tender. Stir in remaining ingredients. Reduce heat to low; simmer until warmed through, 10 to 15 minutes. Serves 15.

Crunchy Taco Coleslaw

Debie Pindral
Painesdale, MI

I always make this yummy coleslaw for potlucks and picnics...it's so simple to fix, yet everyone loves it.

16-oz. pkg. coleslaw mix
8-oz. pkg. shredded
   Mexican-blend cheese
1 to 2 tomatoes, chopped

16-oz. bottle western salad
   dressing
7-oz. pkg. nacho cheese tortilla
   chips, crushed

In a large salad bowl, toss together coleslaw, cheese, tomatoes and salad dressing to taste. Just before serving, stir in crushed chips. Makes 8 to 10 servings.

Tote creamy salads to potlucks the no-spill way...packed in a large plastic zipping bag. When you arrive, simply transfer the salad into a serving bowl.

Cheesy Jalapeño Rice

Connie Wilson
Three Rivers, TX

This rice is always a hit at potlucks...and it comes with a fun story! In 1976, while living in an oil camp, our friend Ruth gave us this recipe. Ruth had gotten it from another camp resident while dating her future husband. The woman who shared the recipe said it was so good that if Ruth made this rice for him, Gary would marry her after eating it. It must have worked...they have been married for forty years now!

2 c. long-cooking rice, uncooked	1 lb. pasteurized process cheese spread, cubed
1 onion, chopped	3 jalapeño peppers, seeded and chopped
1/4 c. oil	
6 c. beef broth	
1/2 c. butter	

In a skillet over medium heat, sauté uncooked rice and onion in oil until onion is tender; drain. Add remaining ingredients to skillet. Cover and cook over low heat until rice is tender and most of the broth is absorbed, about 20 to 25 minutes. Remove from heat; let stand, covered, until remaining broth is absorbed. Serves 12.

Help potluck hosts keep track of dishes by taping a label to the bottom of your casserole dish...be sure to use a waterproof marker and include your name and phone number.

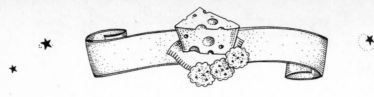

Hamburger Soup

Arlene Crouse
North Lima, OH

During Lent, our church has a soup supper every Wednesday before our Lenten service. This simple soup recipe is a favorite, and it makes plenty to share!

1 lb. ground beef
46-oz. can low-sodium cocktail
   vegetable juice
4 c. water
1.35-oz. pkg. onion soup mix

28-oz. can diced tomatoes,
   drained
3 14-oz. cans mixed vegetables
3 3-oz. pkgs. beef-flavored
   ramen noodles, divided

Brown beef in a large soup pot over medium heat; drain. Add vegetable juice, water, soup mix, tomatoes, undrained vegetables and one to 1-1/2 packets of ramen noodle seasoning. Bring to a boil. Reduce heat to low; cover and simmer for about 20 minutes. Break noodles into small pieces and add to soup. Cook until noodles are tender, 3 to 5 minutes. Serves 12 to 15.

A soup supper menu doesn't need to be fussy and the serving style is "help yourself!" A variety of soups kept warm in slow cookers, along with some rolls and a crock of creamery butter, is all that's needed. No kitchen duty at this gathering...just relax and enjoy each other's company.

Chipped Ham Sandwiches

Carrie Fostor
Baltic, OH

I remember my Grandma Hobart making these sandwiches when we had summertime get-togethers at my grandparents' house. They went so well with her macaroni salad...a tasty way to feed a crowd!

1 c. catsup
1 c. water
2 T. brown sugar, packed
1 T. Worcestershire sauce
1/4 c. vinegar
2 lbs. deli chipped ham
20 to 30 mini sandwich buns, split

In a large saucepan, stir together all ingredients except ham and buns. Cook over medium-low heat for 30 minutes, stirring occasionally. Add ham; stir well and heat through. Serve on buns. Makes 20 to 30 sandwiches.

Big, colorful ice cubes for a party punch bowl...arrange thin slices of citrus or kiwi in muffin tins, fill with water and freeze.

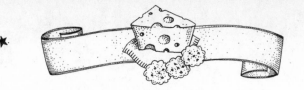

Nana's Loaded Mashed Potatoes

Tia Hamm
Wayland, IA

This is an absolute favorite at our home for special holidays and outdoor cookouts. It's terrific for potlucks too.

12 potatoes, peeled and
   quartered
1/2 lb. bacon, chopped
1/2 c. butter, cubed
1/4 c. sour cream
8-oz. pkg. cream cheese,
   softened

8-oz. pkg. shredded sharp
   Cheddar cheese
1/2 c. green onions, chopped
salt and pepper to taste
Garnish: additional chopped
   green onions

In a stockpot over medium-high heat, cover potatoes with water. Bring to a boil over high heat and cook until fork-tender, 15 to 20 minutes. Drain well. While potatoes are cooking, cook bacon in a skillet over medium heat until crisp. Drain bacon on paper towels. Mash potatoes with butter and sour cream until creamy. Stir in bacon, cheeses, green onions, salt and pepper. Top with a sprinkle of green onions. Serves 8 to 10.

For a party or potluck, roll up sets of flatware in table napkins and place in a shallow tray. An easy do-ahead for the hostess...guests will find it simple to pull out individual sets too.

Speedy Potluck & Party Foods

Darlene's German Potato Salad

Darlene Neeley
Byrdstown, TN

While living in Germany, I came to love the local style of potato salad, made of potatoes, onion, oil, vinegar and a spice that looked like paprika. When I returned to the US, I couldn't find the spice, so I left it out. One day I didn't have enough oil, so I added Italian salad dressing instead...and it tasted just like the potato salad I remembered from Germany! Now my family & friends love this recipe too.

16-oz. bottle Italian salad
   dressing
1 onion, chopped

5 lbs. potatoes
salt and pepper to taste

Pour whole bottle of salad dressing, or to taste, into a large bowl; add onion and let stand. Cover whole potatoes with water in a stockpot. Bring to a boil over medium-high heat; boil potatoes for 15 to 20 minutes, until fork-tender. Drain; let cool slightly, then peel and slice potatoes. Add potatoes to dressing mixture while still warm; toss to coat. Season with salt and pepper. Serve warm or cool. Serves 20.

Easiest-ever sandwiches for a get-together...a big platter of cold cuts and cheese, a basket of fresh breads and a choice of condiments so guests can make their own. Add some chips plus cookies for dessert...done!

Pretty Party Salad

Diana Riggleman
Mansfield, OH

A colorful, yummy, make-ahead salad for picnics. The combination of sweet onion and raisins is a scrumptious surprise!

16-oz. pkg. broccoli and
  cauliflower flowerets
1 c. carrots, peeled and
  shredded

2 c. red cabbage, shredded
1/2 to 1 sweet onion, chopped
1/2 c. raisins
16-oz. bottle coleslaw dressing

Combine all ingredients in a large serving bowl; toss to mix. Cover and chill for at least 2 hours. Stir before serving. Serves 6 to 8.

Plan a recipe swap for your next school potluck or church social! Ask everyone to bring extra copies of the recipe for his or her dish, then slip the copies into resealable plastic bags for protection. Each guest can go home with new favorites.

Italian Bowtie Pasta Salad

Donna Lewis
Ostrander, OH

Everyone enjoys this hearty salad. Other items such as green pepper, onion and pepperoni can be added too.

16-oz. pkg. bowtie pasta, uncooked
1/2 lb. hard salami or Genoa salami, cubed
1/2 lb. deli ham, cubed
1-pt. container cherry tomatoes
4-oz. can sliced black olives, drained
2 8-oz. bottles Italian salad dressing

Cook pasta according to package directions, being careful not to overcook. Drain pasta; rinse with cold water. In a large serving bowl, combine cooked pasta, salami, ham, tomatoes and olives. Drizzle with salad dressing to taste; toss to mix. Cover and refrigerate until serving time. Makes 15 servings.

Keep salads chilled...simply nestle the serving bowl
into a larger bowl filled with crushed ice.

22-Second Salad

*Penny Graham
Rowlett, TX*

A big hit with the Bunco™ gang...they're always asking me to make it again. Quick, easy and delicious!

16-oz. pkg. 3-color coleslaw mix
10-oz. pkg. frozen peas, thawed
1/2 c. red onion, diced

1/2 c. dry-roasted sunflower
  seeds

Combine all ingredients in a large bowl; cover and chill. Make Poppy Seed Dressing ahead of time to allow flavors to blend. At serving time, drizzle with salad dressing; toss to mix. Serves 8 to 12.

Poppy Seed Dressing:

1 c. canola oil
1/2 c. cider vinegar
1/2 c. sugar
2 T. poppy seed

2 t. dry mustard
1 t. salt
1 t. onion powder

Mix ingredients together in a covered container; shake to dissolve sugar. Refrigerate until ready to serve.

Lemony iced tea is so refreshing! Easy to double or triple for a crowd too. Add 9 teabags to 3 quarts boiling water. Let stand for 5 minutes, then discard teabags. Stir in a 12-ounce can of frozen lemonade concentrate and sweeten to taste. Serve over ice...ahh!

Stir & Go Fruit Salad

Marilyn Morel
Keene, NH

This is so easy, yummy and refreshing! Everyone at our church potlucks loves this salad. You can use any flavor gelatin mix to fit the occasion...try strawberry gelatin with strawberries or lime gelatin with pears. The sky's the limit!

3-oz. pkg. orange gelatin mix
8-oz. can crushed pineapple,
   drained
16-oz. container cottage cheese

11-oz. can mandarin oranges,
   drained
8-oz. container frozen whipped
   topping, thawed

Empty dry gelatin mix into a large bowl; stir in pineapple and cottage cheese. Mix until gelatin is dissolved. Stir in oranges. Gently fold in whipped topping; stir until blended. Cover; refrigerate until serving time. Makes 8 to 10 servings.

Frozen Fruit Cups

Teresa Potter
Branson, MO

A friend gave me this recipe after serving it at a ladies' tea. It's a really easy make-ahead recipe...no last-minute fuss!

16-oz. can fruit cocktail
2 to 3 bananas, sliced
1 t. lemon juice
2/3 c. mayonnaise

8-oz. container frozen whipped
   topping, thawed
Garnish: maraschino cherries

In a bowl, combine undrained fruit cocktail, bananas and lemon juice. Stir in mayonnaise and whipped topping. Spoon mixture into 12 paper-lined muffin cups; top each with a cherry. Place muffin tin in freezer. Once frozen, individual cups may be placed in plastic freezer bags and stored in the freezer for several weeks. To serve, arrange on a serving tray and let stand at room temperature 10 to 15 minutes. Makes 12 servings.

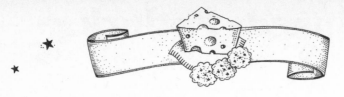

Tropical Snack Mix

Nancy Diem
East Earl, PA

Each Christmas I like to give small ribbon-tied bags of this crisp,
sweet snack mix to friends. It's terrific for parties year 'round too!

8 c. bite-size crispy corn cereal
   squares
2 c. dried pineapple chunks
2 c. dried banana slices
1 c. sweetened dried cranberries

1 c. sliced almonds
1/4 c. butter, melted
1/4 c. sugar
1/4 c. frozen pineapple juice
   concentrate

In a large microwave-safe bowl, toss together cereal, fruit and nuts. In
a separate small bowl, mix remaining ingredients; drizzle over cereal
mixture. Microwave, uncovered, on high setting for 5 minutes,
stirring every 2 minutes. Spread on wax paper to dry. Store in an
airtight container. Makes about 14 cups.

Paper baking cups are perfect for serving up party-size scoops
of nuts or snack mix. They come in lots of colors and patterns
too...you're sure to find one to suit your occasion.

Speedy Potluck & Party Foods

Sweet-and-Sourdough Nuggets

Kathy Grashoff
Fort Wayne, IN

Turn a bag of pretzel nuggets into a tasty treat...it takes just a few minutes and some common pantry ingredients!

15-oz. pkg. sourdough pretzel
   nuggets
2/3 c. oil

1/3 c. sugar
1 to 2 t. cinnamon

Place pretzel nuggets in a large microwave-safe bowl; set aside. Combine remaining ingredients in a small bowl; pour over pretzel nuggets and toss to coat. Microwave, uncovered, on high setting for 2 minutes; stir. Microwave an additional 3 to 4 minutes until oil is absorbed, stirring after each minute. Cool to room temperature. Store in an airtight container. Makes 12 to 16 servings.

Need a crunchy snack for a crowd? Pop up a big bowl of popcorn, then toss it with butter and a savory pizza-flavored sprinkle. For 8 cups popcorn, combine 1/4 cup grated Parmesan cheese, 2 teaspoons Italian seasoning, 2 teaspoons paprika, one teaspoon onion powder and one teaspoon garlic powder. Add salt to taste and mix well...yum!

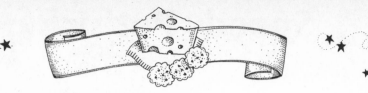

Spinach Party Puffs

Vickie

We love these flavorful bite-size morsels! The unbaked puffs can even be frozen...no need to thaw before baking. Terrific for last-minute celebrations!

10-oz. pkg. frozen chopped spinach
1/2 c. onion, chopped
2 eggs, lightly beaten
1/2 c. grated Parmesan cheese
1/2 c. shredded Cheddar cheese

1/2 c. blue cheese salad dressing
1/4 c. butter, melted and slightly cooled
1/8 t. garlic powder
8-1/2 oz. pkg. cornbread mix

In a saucepan, cook spinach according to package directions, adding onion at the same time. Drain spinach well and press out any excess liquid; set aside. In a large bowl, combine remaining ingredients except cornbread mix. Add spinach mixture and dry cornbread mix; stir well. Cover and chill until firm; form dough into one-inch balls. Cover and chill until serving time. Place chilled puffs on an ungreased baking sheet. Bake at 350 degrees for 10 to 12 minutes, until lightly golden. Makes about 5 dozen.

For stand-up parties, make it easy for guests by serving foods that can be eaten in just one or two bites.

Oven Cheesy Bread

Jasmine Burgess
East Lansing, MI

This is a recipe that I tweaked to make it easier and more to my family's tastes. It's so good with chili and anything Italian...my husband asks for it often.

1 loaf Italian bread, sliced
    1 to 1-1/2 inches thick
1/2 c. butter, softened
1 t. salt
2 T. dried parsley

2 t. smoked paprika
1 t. garlic powder
1/2 t. onion powder
1-1/2 c. shredded Cheddar or
    Mexican-blend cheese

Lay out bread slices on a greased or parchment paper-lined baking sheet. In a bowl, blend butter with seasonings until it forms a smooth paste. Spread each slice of bread with one tablespoon butter mixture; top with 3 tablespoons cheese. Bake at 350 degrees for 5 to 7 minutes, until cheese is melted and bubbly. Makes 8 to 10 servings.

An instant appetizer that's sure to be a hit! Unwrap a block of cream cheese and place it on a serving plate. Top with spicy pepper sauce or fruity chutney. Serve with crisp crackers and a cheese spreader.

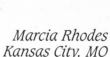

Very Best Texas Caviar

Marcia Rhodes
Kansas City, MO

*A most-requested appetizer at every potluck and
family gathering that I attend.*

16-oz. can black-eyed peas,
  drained and rinsed
16-oz. can pinto beans, drained
  and rinsed
15-oz. can shoepeg corn,
  drained
2-oz. jar sliced pimentos,
  drained

1 c. celery, chopped
1 c. green pepper, chopped
1-1/2 t. jalapeño peppers,
  chopped
Optional: 1/2 c. onion, chopped
tortilla chips

Combine all ingredients except tortilla chips in a large serving bowl;
toss to mix. Pour cooled Vinegar Sauce over vegetable mixture. For
best flavor, cover and chill overnight. Use a slotted spoon to serve
with tortilla chips. Makes 8 to 10 servings.

Vinegar Sauce:

1/2 c. oil
3/4 c. cider vinegar
1 T. water

1 c. sugar
1 t. salt
1/2 t. pepper

Mix all ingredients in a small saucepan over medium heat. Bring to a
boil; allow to boil for 2 minutes. Cool.

A festive container for chips in a jiffy! Simply tie a knot in each corner
of a brightly colored bandanna, then tuck a bowl into the center.

Can't-Miss Pimento Cheese

Brenda Hughes
Houston, TX

This spread is so much fresher tasting than store-bought! It goes a long way too. Serve it with corn chips or on slices of bread...yum!

8-oz. pkg. finely shredded sharp
   Cheddar cheese
8-oz. pkg. finely shredded white
   Cheddar cheese

4-oz. jar sliced pimentos
1/2 c. mayonnaise
salt and pepper to taste

In a bowl, mix cheeses and undrained pimentos. Stir in mayonnaise until well-blended. Add salt and pepper to taste; stir again. Cover and refrigerate until serving time. Serves 8 to 10.

Homemade Hummus

Fran Akkaway
Parsippany, NJ

This hummus recipe has been in our family for many years. Whenever someone has a get-together, they always ask me to make the hummus and "please bring some string cheese too." Best part, it's a healthy treat. I hope you love it too!

19-oz. can chickpeas, drained
   and rinsed
1/2 c. tahini paste or creamy
   peanut butter
1/2 c. canola oil

1/2 c. lemon juice
1 t. garlic powder
1 t. salt
pita wedges, string cheese

Add all ingredients except pita wedges and string cheese to a blender. Blend until smooth; transfer to a shallow bowl. Serve with pita wedges and string cheese for dipping. Makes 8 to 10 servings.

Fill up a big party tray with fresh veggies for dipping and snacking...calorie-counting friends will thank you!

Old-Fashioned Butterscotch Bars

Summer Staib
Broomfield, CO

One day I was looking for something new to bake and found this recipe. It was an instant winner...a rich butterscotch flavor and so easy to make!

1/2 c. butter, melted and slightly
   cooled
2 c. self-rising flour
1-3/4 c. brown sugar, packed

2 eggs, beaten
1 t. vanilla extract
1 c. chopped pecans
Garnish: powdered sugar

In a large bowl, combine melted butter, flour, brown sugar and eggs; mix well. Stir in vanilla and pecans. Spread in a 13"x9" baking pan sprayed with non-stick vegetable spray. Bake at 350 degrees for 15 to 20 minutes, until a toothpick inserted into the center tests clean. Cool completely. Dust with powdered sugar and cut into bars. Makes about 2 dozen.

Keep ingredients on hand for a yummy, quick-fix dessert. A real life-saver whenever you receive a last-minute potluck invitation or your child announces, "Mom, there's a bake sale...tomorrow!"

Better Than Brownies

Gladys Kielar
Perrysburg, OH

*If you love brownies, you'll like these baked goodies even better!
These are so easy and always come out right. They are a favorite
at our teacher staff meetings.*

3.4-oz. pkg. cook & serve
  chocolate pudding mix
2 c. milk
18-1/2 oz. pkg. chocolate cake
  mix

1 c. semi-sweet chocolate chips
1 c. chopped nuts

Prepare dry pudding mix with milk according to package directions;
cook until slightly thickened. Remove from heat. Stir in dry cake mix.
Spread batter in a greased 13"x9" baking pan; sprinkle with chocolate
chips and nuts. Bake at 350 degrees for 30 minutes. Cool; cut into
squares. Makes about 2 dozen.

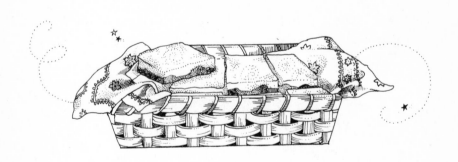

Oversize cookie bars are tempting, but for a change,
slice them into one-inch squares and set them in frilly
paper candy cups. Guests will feel free to sample
"just a bite" of several different treats.

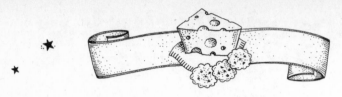

Fluffy Lemon-Raspberry Dessert

Jana Wilson
Laramie, WY

This lemony dessert is just wonderful! Make it ahead of time so the different layers have time to cool. It's delightful made with blueberry jam too.

16-1/2 oz. tube refrigerated
    sugar cookie dough
3 T. all-purpose flour
12-oz. pkg. white chocolate
    chips
16-oz. container lemon frosting

8-oz. pkg. cream cheese,
    softened
8-oz. container frozen whipped
    topping, thawed
1 t. lemon extract
3/4 c. seedless raspberry jam

Break up cookie dough into a bowl; knead in flour until mixed well. Press dough into the bottom of a greased 13"x9" baking pan. Bake at 350 degrees for about 15 minutes, until golden. Remove from oven; immediately sprinkle with chocolate chips. When chips are glossy and softened, spread with a spatula. Refrigerate. In a separate bowl, beat together frosting, cream cheese and whipped topping. Add extract; mix well. Chill frosting mixture until baked crust has completely cooled; spread over crust. Microwave jam briefly; drizzle jam over frosting layer. Refrigerate until set; cut into squares. Makes 12 to 15 servings.

Bake up some ice cream cone cupcakes for a school party. Prepare a cake mix and fill 24 flat-bottom cones 2/3 full of batter. Set the cones in muffin tins and bake as package directs for cupcakes. Let cool, then add frosting and lots of candy sprinkles. Kids will love 'em!

Pineapple Sheet Cake

Teresa Moore
Pawhuska, OK

I first tried this cake at a church supper. It was so good, I went back for seconds! Try it and you'll agree.

2 c. all-purpose flour
2 c. sugar
2 t. baking soda
1 t. vanilla extract

2 eggs, beaten
20-oz. can crushed pineapple
Optional: chopped pecans

In a large bowl, combine flour, sugar, baking soda, vanilla, eggs and undrained pineapple. Mix well. Spread batter in a greased and floured 15"x10" jelly-roll pan. Bake at 325 degrees for 30 minutes, until cake tests done with a toothpick. Spread with Cream Cheese Frosting while still warm. Sprinkle with pecans, if desired. Cool; cut into squares. Makes 15 to 20 servings.

Cream Cheese Frosting:

8-oz. pkg. cream cheese, softened
1/2 c. margarine, softened

1 t. vanilla extract
1 c. powdered sugar

In a large bowl, blend all ingredients together until smooth.

A compromise is the art of dividing a cake in such a way that everyone believes that he has got the biggest piece.
– Paul Gauguin

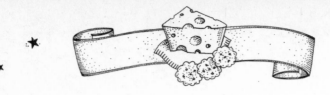

Dinner Theater Dessert

Dani Simmers
Kendallville, IN

A wonderful make-ahead dessert that can be either chocolate or lemon flavored! Two of my children were in theater during their high school years. This dessert was always served at the "Backstage Dinner Theater" productions, hence the name.

1 c. all-purpose flour
1/2 c. margarine, softened
3/4 c. chopped pecans, divided
8-oz. pkg. cream cheese,
    softened
1 c. powdered sugar

8-oz. container frozen whipped
    topping, thawed and divided
2 3-1/2 oz. pkgs. instant
    chocolate or lemon pudding
    mix
3 c. milk

In a bowl, combine flour, margarine and 1/2 cup pecans. Mix well; press into the bottom of an ungreased 13"x9" baking pan. Bake at 350 degrees for 10 to 15 minutes; allow to cool. In a separate bowl, combine cream cheese, powdered sugar and one cup whipped topping; spread over baked layer. Whisk together dry pudding mixes and milk according to package directions; pour over cream cheese layer. Cover and chill for at least one hour. Spread with remaining whipped topping; sprinkle with remaining pecans. Cover and chill for one hour to overnight. Cut into squares. Makes 24 servings.

Toting along a sheet cake? Make sure the frosting will still look party-perfect when you arrive. Insert toothpicks halfway into the cake before covering in plastic wrap...they'll keep the plastic wrap from touching the frosting.

Index

Appetizers

Breads

Desserts

Mains

Index

Salads

Sandwiches

Index

Have a taste for more?

We created our official Circle of Friends so we could
fill everyone in on the latest scoop at once.
Visit us online to join in the fun and discover free
recipes, exclusive giveaways and much more!

www.gooseberrypatch.com

Join Our Circle of Friends

Find us on Facebook

Follow us on twitter

Read Our Blog

Call us toll-free at 1·800·854·6673

U.S. to Canadian recipe equivalents

Volume Measurements

1/4 teaspoon	1 mL
1/2 teaspoon	2 mL
1 teaspoon	5 mL
1 tablespoon = 3 teaspoons	15 mL
2 tablespoons = 1 fluid ounce	30 mL
1/4 cup	60 mL
1/3 cup	75 mL
1/2 cup = 4 fluid ounces	125 mL
1 cup = 8 fluid ounces	250 mL
2 cups = 1 pint =16 fluid ounces	500 mL
4 cups = 1 quart	1 L

Weights

1 ounce	30 g
4 ounces	120 g
8 ounces	225 g
16 ounces = 1 pound	450 g

Oven Temperatures

300° F	150° C
325° F	160° C
350° F	180° C
375° F	190° C
400° F	200° C
450° F	230° C

Baking Pan Sizes

Square

8x8x2 inches	2 L = 20x20x5 cm
9x9x2 inches	2.5 L = 23x23x5 cm

Rectangular

13x9x2 inches	3.5 L = 33x23x5 cm

Loaf

9x5x3 inches	2 L = 23x13x7 cm

Round

8x1-1/2 inches	1.2 L = 20x4 cm
9x1-1/2 inches	1.5 L = 23x4 cm